A PICTORIAL RECORD OF THE FIRST FLEET RE-ENACTMENT VOYAGE

Sailing Home

1788 1988

ANGUS
& ROBERTSON
PUBLISHERS

PHOTOGRAPHS MALCOLM CLARKE   TEXT DAVID IGGULDEN

to
Henrik Bak Nielsen, aged 25,
lost at sea 22 August 1987

*Special thanks to Jonathan King, Wally
Franklin and the First Fleet crews, and to
those from London to Sydney who
supported the voyage.*

*Thanks also to the following for use of
their photographs: The* Argus, *Cape
Town: page 13; page 76 ; page 77.
Leon Faivre: page 111, top.
Peter W. Galton: page 88; page 89; page
90; page 91; page 92, left and top; page
93, bottom; page 94, right; page 99, left; page 110.
Tony Lewis and the Adelaide* Advertiser:
*page 29, top; page 30, top right and
bottom; page 31; page 35, top.
Rodney Hearne (Sydney Photos): page 95, top.
Annette Parkes: page 98; page 108,
bottom left ; page 109, left.*

The illustrations on page 114 are from
Ships That Shaped Australia *by Jack
L. Koskie, published by Angus & Robertson.*

ANGUS & ROBERTSON PUBLISHERS

*Unit 4, Eden Park, 31 Waterloo Road,
North Ryde, NSW, Australia 2113, and
16 Golden Square, London W1R 4BN,
United Kingdom*

*First published in Australia
by Angus & Robertson Publishers in 1988*

*Photographs Copyright © Malcolm Clarke, 1988
Text Copyright © David Iggulden, 1988*

*National Library of Australia
Cataloguing-in-publication data*

*Clarke, Malcolm 1951-
    Sailing home: a pictorial record of the First Fleet
    Re-enactment voyage.
    ISBN 0 207 15965 3.*

*1. First Fleet Re-enactment — Pictorial works.
2. Voyages and travels. 3. Seafaring life.
4. Australia — Centennial celebrations etc.
I. Iggulden, David, 1949-   . II. Title.*

910.4

*Typeset in Times and Frutiger by The Type Shop
Printed in Australia by Owen King Printers*

CONTENTS

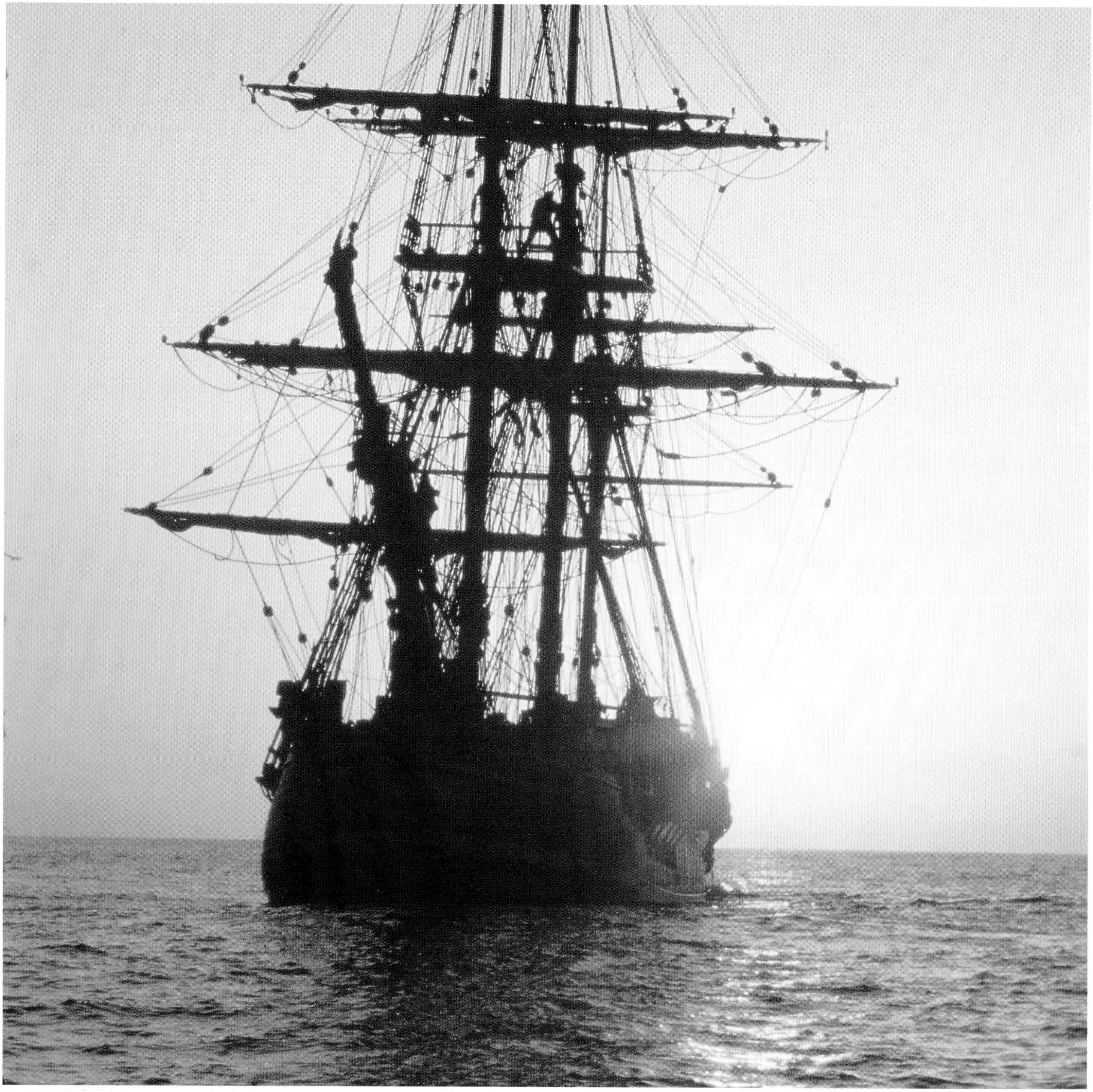

THE VOYAGES

1787-1788

Just before first light on 13 May 1787, in the seventeenth year of the reign of King George III, a fleet of small wooden sailing vessels weighed anchor in the morning mist of rural England and dropped quietly down Solent Water.

Criticised and condemned by the few who knew of their passing, 1350 seamen, marines and convicts set sail for an utterly unknown continent on the other side of the world, to found a new nation in which no European had ever before lived.

By midday all the ships had passed the Needles and the afternoon saw them in the English Channel sailing before a moderate sou'easterly breeze. Thirty-seven weeks later they anchored in Port Jackson, Sydney.

This was the First Fleet.

Two centuries later, early in our age of space exploration, the only equivalent enterprise would be a colonisation of the moon. Just as Abel Tasman and James Cook sailed where no man had dared in the 17th and 18th centuries, so Russia and America today are venturing into space. As Tasman sighted Australasia and Cook landed at Botany Bay, so Gagarin was the first man in space and Armstrong the first to step upon the moon.

The First Fleet of 1787 was the greatest migratory voyage attempted by man. It travelled further than any other migratory passage, it carried more people, and it went to a land about which the voyagers' ignorance was total.

What is more, it was successful.

All eleven ships, of which the largest was only about 35 metres long and the smallest just a little over 21 metres, arrived at Botany Bay within three days of each other after eight months at sea. Even for those times the vessels were small — the flagship, HMS *Sirius*, was only half the size of an average merchant ship of the East India Company—and not one of them had been designed to transport convicts or stores on a voyage of this length.

Only 48 people died during the voyage, an amazing achievement in an age of malnutrition, appalling living conditions, medical ignorance, and low value on human life (the expression "may as well be hanged for a sheep as a lamb" comes from these times when theft of livestock was a capital offence). The Second Fleet — which sailed from England at the end of 1789 — lost 267 people.

The settlement that the First Fleet established in Port Jackson survived to spread and grow ultimately into the modern Commonwealth of Australia. For the government in Britain and for the commander, Captain Phillip, the achievements of the First Fleet were unparalleled. The first settlement attempts in North America, for example — a mere 4800 kilometres across the Atlantic from Britain — ended in starvation and disaster. Yet here was the First Fleet, a year and half's communication from home, making a success of it. It was a magnificent feat of seamanship, navigation and organisation.

The actual decision to send the Fleet was taken in London on 19 August 1786. But why to Australia at all? After the inept debacle of the American Wars of 1776-83 Britain lost her traditional penal colony, and with the harsh laws of the times her prisons were soon overflowing with petty felons. Hulks from the Royal Navy were rigged-down and converted to floating prisons to absorb some of the convicts, but the government under 21-year-old William Pitt was searching for a long term solution to the problem.

Some ministers advocated hanging the felons. But the more humane Pitt, acting on information from Captain Cook's botanist, Sir Joseph Banks, adopted the alternative solution of transporting them to a new penal colony in New South Wales. A settlement there would also forestall any French or Dutch claims to the continent, and help reaffirm Britain as a colonial power after the loss of her American colony.

Shortly after the decision was taken the Admiralty had notices posted in the merchant coffee houses of London (coffee houses from which Lloyds' Underwriters began operating) advertising for suitable vessels for the enterprise. Within two weeks five transport ships for the convicts — the barques *Alexander, Charlotte* and *Scarborough*, the ship *Lady Penrhyn*, and the brig *Friendship* — and three storeships for the new settlement — the full-rigged barques *Golden Grove, Fishburn* and *Borrowdale* — had been chartered. HMS *Sirius* was commissioned in October as flagship with HMS *Supply* as her armed tender, and another vessel, the ship *Prince of Wales*, was chartered in January as the sixth transport. The original departure date had been set for mid-October; that the Fleet didn't finally depart until more than six months later shows the initial lack of planning by the Home Office.

Captain Arthur Phillip RN was selected as the Fleet and colony commanding officer, a choice that raised a few eyebrows even within the Admiralty. But amongst his various skills Phillip had experience in transporting convicts before, was a qualified surveyor, came of farming stock and so could help establish the settlement, and had previously sailed to South America and the Cape, both stops along the planned route to New South Wales.

He had also been a spy for the government and, given the mood of revolution in continental Europe and the recent setback to Britain's empire in the Americas, this experience may well have helped his appointment. At any rate, although Phillip may not have been an inspired commander, his choice for this expedition certainly was.

Meanwhile, as the Fleet was being prepared, the press of the day attacked the organisers and the conditions on the ships in broadsheets circulated in and around London. An anti-Fleet lobby was formed, led by Lord George Gordan, one of the leading campaigners for penal reform in Georgian Britain. He debated the issue of the new penal colony publicly, and even circulated a petition to prevent the expedition from sailing.

But the First Fleet eventually departed from Portsmouth on 13 May 1787, calling at Santa Cruz de Tenerife, Rio de Janeiro, Cape Town, Botany Bay, and anchoring off Sydney Cove in Port Jackson on 26 January 1788. Phillip followed the trade winds down the Atlantic and picked up the westerlies across the Southern Ocean to pass south of Tasmania, averaging 132 kilometres a day. This route is the traditional passage for sailing vessels, and the grain and wheat clippers of the 19th century crossed the same seas.

Some idea of the conditions on board the ships is given by *Scarborough*, where 208 convicts plus crew and marines shared her cramped spaces. A fortnight after leaving England the convicts attempted to seize the ship, but this uprising and later ones were put down. *Scarborough* also sailed with the Second Fleet, the only First Fleet ship to return to the colony.

The *Lady Penrhyn, Charlotte, Friendship* and *Prince of Wales* all carried female convicts, and in these ships the sailors and marines frequently broke through the wooden bulkheads into the women's quarters. Some were invited and some were not, and many were flogged for their actions, including the women. The children that resulted became the first generation of Australian-born settlers.

1987-1988

Since that epic voyage two hundred years ago the new nation of Australia has changed dramatically; Britain is now only a three week sea passage away, or a twelve hour flight by supersonic Concorde — or a mere twenty second telephone call.

There are as many ways to celebrate the passing of these years as there are Australians but, whatever the idea or dream, it takes vision to turn it into substance. One such Australian with this vision is Jonathan King, descendant of Lieutenant Philip King RN (Phillip's aide-de-campe in 1787),whose dream was to re-create that amazing voyage of two hundred years ago.

The First Fleet Re-enactment is the largest fleet of sailing ships to sail together since the Crimean War of 1854. It is the largest multi-national fleet of ships ever to sail together in peace time, comprising vessels from Britain, Australia, New Zealand, Canada, Norway, Sweden and the Netherlands. And its crews of various religions and cultures total over twenty-five different nationalities, making it one of the most internationally diverse expeditions. It is, quite simply, the greatest marine re-enactment ever attempted.

Eight First Fleet Re-enactment ships sailed together for more than nine months across 32,000 kilometres of the loneliest and emptiest stretches of ocean in the world, re-creating the most extraordinary marine enterprise ever conceived. Basically following the same route of 1787-88, the passage was still — to the surprise of many of the crew — a very difficult one. It was physically and mentally demanding, and it was dangerous in the extreme — in fact, deadly. But there are other parallels with the original voyage.

This Bicentennial celebration was subject to virulent, often caustic, criticism from individuals and official bodies within Australia, from its inception in 1977 right up to its arrival in Sydney eleven years later. As in 1787, the organisers were the target of an anti-Fleet campaign; the project was lampooned as crazy and impracticable. But through sheer bloody-mindedness, determination, and faith, a second First Fleet of square-rigged sailing ships slipped down the Solent on 13 May 1987 and dropped anchor again off Farm Cove on 26 January 1988, two hundred years later to the day. The bloody-mindedness belongs to the First Fleet Re-enactment creator, Jonathan King; the determination to director, Wally Franklin; and the faith to the owners, masters and crews of the First Fleet Re-enactment ships.

Further support came with the appointment of the Honorary President of the expedition, explorer and conservationist Thor Heyerdahl, of *Kon Tiki* and *Ra* fame. In 1985 Sir Edmund Hillary, the first man to climb Everest, joined the legendary Alan Villiers as another of the Fleet patrons. And then after support from two successive Prime Ministers — Malcolm Fraser and Bob Hawke — Buckingham Palace became involved.

Her Majesty the Queen agreed to review the Fleet off Portsmouth and to signal their departure for Australia, while in a letter to the ships Prince Philip wrote: "They carry with them the very best of wishes of the 'Old Country' for the success of the commemoration of the inaugural event in the founding of modern Australia."

The re-enactment was a majestic and exhausting experience for all involved. The effort needed to create and sustain a privately financed marine expedition of this magnitude would indicate that it will be the last for a long time, perhaps for ever. Certainly Australia is unlikely to see its like again. Yet it has introduced a thousand people around the world to the demands and rewards of square-sail training. No words can convey the sheer exhilaration and simple beauty of sailing on a square-rigged sailing ship, of making a landfall on an unknown foreign coast at night, and even of climbing a swaying wooden mast thirty metres above the deck with the wind whipping hair across your face. The second First Fleet has given this experience to as many as it could, and if measured by no other yardstick than this the expedition has been a worthwhile success.

The wheels did almost fall off when the Fleet reached Brazil in August 1987; put brutally, the money was running out. The Australian Bicentennial Authority had lent the Australian First Fleet Re-enactment Company A$500,000 in London in April 1987. But that was to be the lot. Although the eight Fleet ships are flying the Australian flag around the world, with over 70 per cent Australian crews, further hoped-for sponsorship and bicentennial aid did not eventuate, and for a desperate fortnight it seemed that some of the ships would have to turn back — a tragedy after having come so far. But a rescue operation mounted in Australia by Radio 2GB of Sydney alerted the public to the potential disaster. From private donations and other support the Fleet survived the crisis, and the ships left Rio on time.

Then on 22 August tragedy struck. At 0120 an urgency signal on the radio was heard by *Tradewind, R. Tucker Thompson* and *Soren Larsen. Anna Kristina* had lost a man overboard. The vessels immediately altered course and closed on *Anna Kristina*. At first it was not clear who had gone over the side, but then it was confirmed that it was First Mate Henrik Nielsen.

The wind was east-nor'east force 4 gusting 5, with moderate seas on a moderate swell. *Tradewind* reached *Anna Kristina* in an hour, then *R. Tucker Thompson* joined her and *Soren Larsen* arrived before dawn. Searchlights and Aldis signalling lamps swept the sea until first light, at which time Commodore Mike Kichenside instigated a box-search in the grey dawn. The sea and winds abated but it was very cold. All hands were posted on lookout around the decks, in the rigging and up the masts. Every sighting was investigated, and many drifting fishing buoys, plastic containers and bottles were found.

Ironically, Henrik had been setting another headsail because the wind was easing. As he took the sheet to a belaying pin to haul in on the clew, a gust filled the flapping sail and flipped him over the side. He clung on for a while but the ship was making 5 to 6 knots, and when he let go he drifted away into the night. Lifebelts were thrown to him and Johan Brox dived overboard to try to swim to him. Johan had to be hauled back when he too was in danger of drowning in the lumpy seas.

The search continued during the cold day. In the afternoon the search area was extended. By dusk, at 1835, it was apparent to all the Masters and the Commodore that because of the temperature of the water and the length of time since he went overboard — 17 hours — there was no hope Henrik could still be alive. The search was stopped.

At 2000 the four ships, lit by their green and red running lights, gathered together in the now quiet sea and each held their own short service in the dark.

The Fleet sailed on towards Africa minus one friend, and all involved acutely more aware of how dangerous a venture they had undertaken.

As happened two hundred years ago the voyage really started before 13 May. The first ships began to gather in London in early April 1987 when the smallest in the Fleet, the *R. Tucker/Thompson*, berthed in the period setting of St Katherine's-by-the-Tower dock. She was soon followed by *Soren Larsen,* which warped through the narrow lock about the middle of the month.

The largest vessel of the Fleet, the *Amorina,* had to moor outside in the river at Tower Pier, and the next to enter St Katherine's was the Dutch registered *Tradewind.* The British barque, *Kaskelot,* which was sailing with the Fleet only until 14 May, also moored alongside Tower Pier. *Bounty, Anna Kristina* and *Our Svanen* would join at the final rendezvous at Portsmouth; *One and All,* late in completing her fitting-out, would meet them all in mid-Atlantic.

On 27 April the giant arms of Tower Bridge slowly opened upwards, and the graceful square-riggers sailed downriver past hundreds and hundreds of cheering Londoners on an epic journey to the other side of the world.

Søren Larsen

Søren Larsen, flagship of the First Fleet Re-enactment, was built in 1949 by Søren Larsen and Sons in their shipyard at Nykøbing Mørs in northern Denmark. She is a traditional carvel ship of 90 per cent oak-on-beech, and was originally rigged as a galeas with an auxiliary engine. She is built of 75mm oak outer planking on double 175mm oaken frames, and a 60mm inner planking of oak. The whole is through-fastened. As ship number 95 she was one of the last completed at this yard, and was appropriately named after her builder.

Although relatively young, she was designed as a traditional three-hatch single-hold Baltic trader, and until 1972 traded throughout Scandinavia, Britain, northern Europe and even Iceland, carrying general cargo such as timber, wheat and beans. After being laid up and gutted by fire she was bought in 1978 by her present owners, Tony and Robin Davies of Square Sail Britain, and completely refitted. New decks of iroko hardwood were laid, and she was rigged as a late 19th-century brigantine with masts, yards and spars of Douglas Fir from the New Forest. Following the British tradition that changing a ship's name will bring her bad luck, Tony and Robin kept her original name and changed only her flag from Danish to British, re-registering her at the old Roman port of Colchester.

The *Søren Larsen* began working life again in early 1979, and achieved international fame in the classic BBC television series the "Onedin Line". Other film work followed including *The French Lieutenant's Woman* and *In Search of the Marie Celeste,* and in 1982 she sailed north to the pack-ice to become the first wooden sailing ship to reach the Greenland Arctic Circle for seventy years. Here she starred in the BBC television series "Shackleton", playing the roles of three famous ships — the *Endurance, Discovery* and *Nimrod.*

Then followed a charter from 1982 to 1985 with the Jubilee Sailing Trust of Britain, where square-rigged sail training was given jointly to able and physically disabled people of all ages. This pilot scheme with the *Søren Larsen* was so successful that a specially designed vessel was commissioned for this work, and the 52 metre barque *Lord Nelson* now sails out of Southampton. It was during this charter that the ship's builder and name-sake died in Denmark.

The *Søren Larsen* was chartered for the First Fleet Re-enactment Voyage in 1986, and refitted at her Gloucester base by her crew that winter. The Commodore's flag was raised when she reached St Katherine's-by-the-Tower in London in April 1987. When the Re-enactment finishes in June 1988, she will charter and cruise throughout the South Pacific and then return to Britain, perhaps by the Cape Horn.

R. Tucker Thompson

From the second oldest to the second youngest ship of the Fleet — and also a square-topsail schooner — the *R. Tucker Thompson.* This unusual name in fact follows the tradition of the sea, for the vessel is named after square-rig ship owner and skipper, R. Tucker Thompson.

Tucker owned the famous barque *Cartheginian,* a refitted Baltic trader which was sailed by the legendary Alan Villiers and Adrian Small, and used in the film *Hawaii,* but was later sold. Tucker bought and refitted a second Baltic trader, the *Argus,* which he sold and which is still working as a sail training vessel for the Boy Scouts off the Californian coast. He moved to New Zealand from America and began in 1977 to build his own ship with his son, Todd, but died only a year later. Todd continued the building between jobs — one of which was helping rig the *Bounty* at Whangarei, where he and Russell Harris met — and completed the steel hull in 1982.

Todd and Russell — a former farmer and theatre director — formed a partnership that same year, moved the hull to Russell's home at Mangawhai Heads north of Auckland, and finally finished the schooner in 1985. Volunteers from all over New Zealand, but especially from Mangawhai, helped complete the vessel in one way or another, and at the launching on 12 October 1985 over 4000 people attended the naming of the *R. Tucker Thompson.* Elders of the Northland Maori tribes performed a traditional ritual blessing, and presented the small ship with a carving of the Karewa spirit to safeguard her journeyings. This talisman is permanently mounted in the navigation space.

The *R. Tucker Thompson* reflects modern ship-building practices, with a welded steel hull, four watertight bulkheads, and steel plate decks. The topsides, however, are of kwila hardwood, the deck is overlaid with kwila planking, and the masts, yards and spars are of laminated Oregon pine which were originally part of a one-hundred-year-old Auckland warehouse.

After charter and filming the television "Adventure" series in the Bay of Islands, she set sail for England in late 1986 via the South Pacific and Panama to join the Second First Fleet. In February 1987, between Bermuda and the Azores, she ran into a wind of force 12 — a classic north Atlantic hurricane with 80 knot winds and a barometer of 969 millibars. She rode out the storm, suffered no damage, and entered the Thames in April to be the first of the First Fleet Re-enactment ships to arrive in London.

Anna Kristina

The galeas *Anna Kristina* is virtually half the age of modern Australia, and the oldest vessel of the First Fleet Re-enactment by many years. She was built in 1889 as a Hardanger Jakt on a farm at Stanavic in Norway, from a design by a Den Norsk Veritas agent. She was originally named *Dyrafjeld,* and with the other Hardanger Jakts she carried dried fish from northern Norway south to Bergen, returning with general cargo for the port merchants.

Hardanger Jakts were often built on the farms of their owners in the Hardanger region of Norway, and traded in almost every cargo along the coast to the North Sea and into the Baltic. At the turn of the century hundreds of these wooden vessels with their distinctive transoms sailed from Norway, varying in size from 12 to 24 metres on deck and usually rigged as a square-topsail sloop or square-topsail ketch.

They were known to make very fast passages; and sloop-rigged *Dyrafjeld* recorded a passage of just over 600 kilometres in only thirty-four hours shortly after she was launched.

The *Dyrafjeld* traded mainly in dried and salted cod and general cargo, but she sometimes carried timber from Riga in Russia. Her first engine was installed in 1900 — a mere 12 horsepower — and in the late 1920s when the coastal trade was in decline she was sold and rerigged as a galeas — a gaff-rigged square-topsail ketch with a course sail set from the deck. At the beginning of World War II she was rigged down and a bigger engine and wheelhouse fitted aft. She capsized in 1975 when her cargo of timber shifted, and the following year she suffered further damage when she collided with another vessel. This signalled the end of her commercial life and she was laid-up after eighty-six years continuous service with no future. Then, in 1977, Hans and Hetti van de Vooren bought her.

From fittings, equipment and parts from other derelict jakts, they fully restored the broken vessel to an authentic galeas-rigged Hardanger Jakt. Her hull and frames were still sound, but most of the deck and the unique transom had to be replaced. In 1981 *Anna Kristina* was named and the jakt sailed Norwegian waters once again, still under the Norwegian flag.

Charters commenced in 1982, including historical film work and a two year charter to Spitzbergen in the Arctic Circle, but the greatest charter of her hundred-year-old life didn't begin until she sailed into Portsmouth in 1987 to join the Re-enactment Fleet. She now has a new Volvo engine and accommodation for sail trainees in her old holds, and with her brown sails over her dark green and oiled wooden hull she is as pretty a ship as you'll ever see afloat today.

Amorina

Of all the First Fleet vessels, perhaps the *Amorina* has the strangest history. She was originally designed as a lightship for the Swedish maritime authorities operating in the Baltic Sea, with the unromantic name of *Lightship 33*. Built in 1934 at the famous Jotaverken Shipyard at Gothenburg, she spent most of her early life at either station *Sydostbrotten* (Southeast Breakers) or *Nordströmsgrund* (Northern Current Shallows) in the eastern Baltic.

This vessel is also probably the strongest of the Fleet, as she is constructed to Lloyds' Ice Class A1 specifications, with 170 mm riveted Swedish steel plates throughout her hull and an icebreaker bow.

Lightship 33 spent an uneventful working life until she was eventually replaced by the modern Kasun Light Houses (a stressed concrete structure sunk in the required position) and was laid up in Stockholm in about 1970. She lay in port for many years but because of the temperatures of the cold northern waters and the low salinity level, hull deterioration was almost negligible.

Meanwhile, a group of Swedish ship owners had just lost their sailing vessel in an accident in the Mediterranean, and they were looking for a replacement vessel. They bought *Lightship 33* in 1979, formed a new company called Amorina Cruises, and renamed the lightship *Amorina*.

At Aveiro, just south of Lisbon, the old lightship underwent a dramatic conversion beneath the warm Portuguese sun. The large accommodation below decks was extended and improved, while above decks three steel masts over 30 metres high were stepped, a new deckhouse fitted amidships, the original wheelhouse moved for'ard, and a saloon added aft. The new *Amorina* left the shipyard in mid 1983 as a white-hulled barquentine with royals, and immediately entered that year's Cutty Sark Tall Ships race around Spain and Portugal.

After all those years in the Baltic, the sunshine called; she stayed south in the tropics and didn't return to Stockholm until 1985. 1986 saw her as a focal point for the season's sailing at Sandhamn, south of Stockholm, but in the winter her future was changed again when two major contracts were offered to Amorina Cruises. They chose the First Fleet Re-enactment, and in late March with a new crew she left Stockholm again, this time bound for London.

For two weeks after leaving Stockholm she was trapped by the late winter ice on her way south, and was eventually taken in tow by a tug.

In April she sailed up the Thames to moor at Tower Pier. The *Amorina* was set to sail for the southern hemisphere.

Tradewind

This is the second oldest vessel of the First Fleet Re-enactment, and yet she has sailed all her working life under just one flag — Dutch. *Tradewind* was built as a fishing vessel at the old Vuyck Shipyard at Capelle aan den Ijssel in 1911, but her original name is not known. Her hull of riveted steel plates has a plumbed stem (straight up-and-down bow) and a graceful counter stern, and her early life was spent sailing out of Katwijk, fishing the grey waters of the North Sea.

She was originally rigged as a ketch (a rig common to fishing boats from all North Sea countries) with wooden decks and no engine at all. In fact her first engine wasn't fitted until the late 1930s, when she was still fishing the North Sea. A second engine was fitted in 1954 and her life dramatically changed. The traditional small hatches to the fish hold below were widened, and for the next twenty years she traded in general cargo from the Netherlands to the smaller North Sea ports. After passing through a series of owners she was permanently moored at Imuiden near Amsterdam in the early 1970s, when she was reduced to a floating home and her sea-going life appeared to be at an end.

But then in 1979 she changed hands once again, and after an extensive refit lasting until 1984 she became the steel-decked schooner *Aaltje en Willem*. Some charter work followed, yet her future was still doubtful until 1986 when she was sold again, this time to Mark Hammond.

During the middle of winter the vessel was completely rerigged alongside Java Quay in the Amsterdam Docks, and in the spring of 1987 she emerged as the gaff-rigged square-topsail schooner, *Tradewind* — but still registered in the Netherlands.

Tradewind also emerged with the greatest charter of her life, and in April that year she moored alongside the ships of the First Fleet Re-enactment at St Katherine's-by-the-Tower and prepared for her voyage south. After seventy-eight years sailing, this sturdy steel vessel crossed the equator for the first time with yet another different cargo — people. Sail training and expedition charter is her work for the foreseeable future, with a base on the east coast of Australia.

One and All

Australia has a long and respected tradition in sail, from the ultimate ship and barque-rigged giants that raced each other in the grain and wool trades between Australia and Britain to the smaller craft that plied the coastal waters and Bass Strait. At the turn of the century in the South Australian gulfs there were many trading schooners, and it is upon these graceful vessels that the youngest ship in the Fleet, the *One and All*, is based.

She is the only wooden brigantine to be built in Australia this century, and much of the credit must go to historian Dr John Young, whose dream it was to operate a sail training vessel out of South Australia. The keel of ironbark was laid by yachtsman Sir James Hardy on 31 October 1982 at North Haven in Adelaide, and work continued throughout mainly with volunteer craftsmen and labour. It was such enthusiasm for the project and the sea that enabled the vessel to be completed, and her name is a reflection of this ideal.

The hull is 70 per cent celery-top pine and Huon pine from Tasmania on jarra from Western Australia, through-bolted on Oregon frames. Only the knees and mainmasts are of steel to give her added strength. White beechwood from Queensland gives her decks a holystoned appearance, and her topmasts, yards and spars are of Tasmania Oregon.

To enable the *One and All* to navigate the shallow waters of the South Australian creeks and estuaries, two centreboards of laminated tallow wood abaft each mast are used instead of a fixed keel or V-shaped hull. With these centreboards lowered, the vessel's draught measures 4.7 metres, but when they are raised by the hand winches on deck the draught is reduced to only 2.7 metres.

One and All was launched on 1 December 1985 and work then began on her topsides and rig. She is classified as an hermaphrodite brigantine (or "jackass" brigantine) with only two masts on her fore crossed by only lower and topsail yards, although a large course sail is also set from the lower topsail yard to the deck.

On 5 April 1987 *One and All* was commissioned by the Premier of South Australia, John Bannon. That same day was also her day of departure, for she immediately left Port Adelaide for the northern hemisphere to meet the First Fleet Re-enactment ships.

Across the Indian Ocean and through Suez to Gibraltar she sailed, and then turned south in the track of the Fleet to Tenerife. She finally caught the other ships off Rio de Janeiro in August, still on her maiden voyage.

Our Svanen

While most traditional shipyards specialising in wooden sailing vessels were closing down or converting to steel and steam in the first half of the 20th century, yards in Scandinavia were still building commercially viable sailing ships, and building them to last. Another one of these fine vessels still operating today is *Our Svanen*, built at Frederikssund in Denmark in 1922 and which continued trading until 1969.

Like the *Søren Larsen*, she is massively constructed of oak-on-oak, with a 75mm carvel hull on 150mm oaken frames just 150mm apart, and an inner ceiling of 50mm oak planking. The whole is through-fastened, and she was originally rigged as a three masted topsail schooner for the Greenland trade. Most of her commercial life was in fact spent carrying grain around Scandinavia for the Tuborg brewery of Denmark.

Her first engine was not fitted until 1955, when a three cylinder Alpha diesel was installed to make her more commercial. At the end of the 1960s her trading life came to an end. She was purchased privately by Doug and Margaret Havers of Canada and was extensively overhauled and rebuilt where necessary in Denmark. Her flag was transferred to Britain and Stornoway became her new port of registry.

In 1977 she finally put to sea again and sailed through the Kiel Canal to Poole in Dorset where she was rerigged as a barquentine. New masts, yards and spars of Douglas Fir were stepped and raised, and new sails from the famous Cranfield Sail Loft were bent on. Proportionately her rig could be taller, but she was deliberately rigged short for safety.

At the close of 1978 she left England on a 6500 kilometre passage to the west coast of Canada, via the Caribbean and Panama, and nine months later she arrived in Victoria, British Columbia, for the first time. For the next six years she was chartered to the Canadian National Defence Forces as a sail training ship for the Sea Cadets, and this dream charter took her on many international voyages and Tall Ship races.

The Sea Cadet charter finished in 1986 and she was put up for sale in Bermuda. A group of Canadian sailing enthusiasts, C.D.A. Sail Pacific Ltd, bought her, and *Our Svanen* returned to Vancouver for work with Expo 86. The original Alpha was finally replaced by a Caterpillar engine. At the end of the year the vessel raced back through the Panama Canal and across the Atlantic to England, joining the First Fleet at Portsmouth in May 1987.

Bounty

The *Bounty* was built at Whangarei in New Zealand during 1978-79, to the exact external specifications of Captain Bligh's *Bounty* of the infamous 1789 mutiny, and this replica featured in the 1984 De Laurentis film, *Bounty.*

Her building materials come from all over the Commonwealth; the hull is made of Australian steel clad with carvel-laid iroko planks from New Zealand, the decks are of New Zealand tanekaha wood, the laminated masts and the yards and spars are of Canadian pine, the sails are of traditional Scottish flax, and the blocks are of English ash and elm. The figurehead is an Englishwoman in blue riding habit of the period; it is said that Bligh commissioned such a figurehead because he knew from his voyages with Captain Cook that the Tahitians had never seen a white woman, and he wished to show them an image of one.

Although often described as a "fully-rigged ship", *Bounty* is in modern terms a barque, or a full-rigged Cat as the rig was called in the 18th century. She is of similar design to Cook's *Endeavour* and *Resolution* — Bligh served as Sailing Master to Cook on *Resolution* — and it was the success of Cook's voyages that prompted the Admiralty to appoint a similar vessel for Bligh's fatal voyage. The original *Bounty* was built as a northeast English collier in 1772, and although the replica's mizzen masts are crossed with square-sail yards, to be classified as a *ship* rig she should have a mizzen topgallant mast. She has only main and topmasts on her mizzen. Where the original *Bounty* had holds below decks for stores and cargo, the replica has fully equipped engine and generator rooms.

Her hull colours are the traditional colours of Royal Naval ships of the period. These were the forerunner of the famous yellow and black chequered hull of the fighting ships during the Napoleonic Wars, epitomised still by HMS Victory at Portsmouth.

After the 1984 film the vessel was laid-up in Los Angeles until the current owners, Bounty Voyages Limited, bought her in 1986 for the First Fleet Re-enactment. She sailed to Vancouver for a refit, and during the subsequent voyage across the Pacific to Australia more filming took place. *Bounty* played the parts of Cook's vessels for the television series "The Voyages of Captain Cook", and once again played herself for the film "The Island", an account of the sequel to the mutiny on Pitcairn Island.

From Australia *Bounty* sailed through the Suez Canal to England and joined the assembling Second First Fleet at HM Naval Dockyard, Portsmouth, berthing only about 100 metres from HMS *Victory.* A descendant of the mutineers from Pitcairn, Michael Evans, was on board as Able Seaman.

Eye of the Wind

The famous *Eye of the Wind* began life in 1911 at the C. Luhring yard at Brake, in Germany, as an engineless topsail schooner named the *Friedrich.* She traded in salt to South America, hides to Cornwall, and china clay back to Germany twice a year until World War I. In 1923 she was fitted with her first engine and employed in the Baltic and North Sea trades, and even as a fishing vessel off Iceland during the summer months.

Her name was changed to *Adele* in 1935, to *Katherina* in 1936, and again to *Frieda* during World War II, but the iron-hulled vessel continued trading around northern Europe until 1969. Renamed the *Merry,* her aft accommodation caught fire in the Baltic while she was trapped in winter ice, and she finished her last trading voyage being towed to Sweden in the thaw — a seemingly sad end to a sailing vessel that had survived two world wars and the demise of sail. She was laid up in Gothenburg, her sailing days over.

But an Anglo-Australian group, Adventure Under Sail, who had met while sailing the New Endeavour in Australia after the Captain Cook Bicentenary, were looking for their own sailing vessel. They were told of the *Merry* hulk lying in Sweden, and after a winter's inspection bought her on St Valentine's Day in 1973. Years of restoration and refitting followed in Gothenburg and in Faversham, Kent, until in October 1976 the newly-rigged brigantine *Eye of the Wind* slipped quietly down the Faversham creek to the sea and Australia.

She circumnavigated the world from east to west via Panama and Suez, and after refitting at Plymouth in 1978 was chartered as the flagship for "Operation Drake". This took the ship to many varied and lonely places during the two year British expedition for young people of all nationalities.

Through the 1980s *Eye of the Wind* undertook charter and film work in the Pacific area, and underwent a change of rig. Her mainmast is now crossed by three yards, making her an hermaphrodite brig, and in this guise she featured in the films *Savage Islands* and *Shogun.* She joined the First Fleet at Fremantle in December 1987 for the voyage around the Australian coast, bringing the Fleet number to nine for the final leg to Sydney.

SOREN LARSEN

Name: SØREN LARSEN, Flagship
Built: Søren Larsen and Sons,
  Nykøbing, Denmark, 1949
Flag: British/Colchester
Signal letters: GYHN
Rig: late 19th century brigantine
Length overall: 42.7 m
Beam: 7.8 m
Draught: 3.2 m
Mast height: 30.5 m
Sail area: 627 m²
Displacement: 299.7 tonnes
Gross tonnage: 128 tonnes
Nett tonnage: 87.7 tonnes
Engine: B&W Alpha diesel, 240 hp,
  single screw, service speed 7 knots

R.TUCKER THOMSON

Name: R. TUCKER THOMPSON

Built: Todd Thompson and Russell Harris,
Whangarei and Mangawhai Heads, New Zealand, 1985

Flag: New Zealand / Whangarei

Signal letters: ZMA2808

Rig: gaff-rigged square-topsail schooner with three-quarter course

Length overall: 25.9 m

Beam: 4.9 m

Draught: 2.6 m

Mast height: 19.8 m

Sail area: 307 m²

Displacement: 55.9 tonnes

Gross tonnage: 44.7 tonnes

Nett tonnage: 33.5 tonnes

Engine: Ford diesel, 120 hp, service speed 5 knots

AMORINA

Name: AMORINA
Built: Jotaverken Shipyard, Gothenburg, Sweden, 1934
Flag: Swedish/Stockholm
Signal letters: SHUT
Rig: barquentine, with standing yards
Length overall: 34.3 m
Beam: 7.7 m
Draught: 4.5 m
Mast height: 34 m
Sail area: 650 m²
Displacement: 538.5 tonnes
Gross tonnage: 349.5 tonnes
Nett tonnage: 201 tonnes
Engine: Deutch 6 cylinder, 500 hp,
single screw, service speed 6.5 knots

TRADE WIND

Name: TRADEWIND

Flag: Netherlands / Amsterdam

Built: Vuyck Shipyard, Capelle aan den Ijssel, Netherlands, 1911

Signal letters: PC8145

Rig: gaff-rigged square-topsail schooner with running course

Length overall: 37.5 m

Beam: 6.6 m

Draught: 2.9 m

Mast height: 31.1 m

Sail area: 530 m²

Displacement: 223.5 tonnes

Gross tonnage: 109.2 tonnes

Nett tonnage: 51.9 tonnes

Engine: Industrie 3 cylinder, 180 hp, single screw, service speed 6.5 knots

ONE AND ALL

Name: ONE AND ALL

Built: Adelaide, South Australia, 1985

Flag: Australian/Port Adelaide

Signal letters: VKON

Rig: hermaphrodite brigantine

Length overall: 39.4 m

Beam: 8.1 m

Draught: 4.7 m

Mast height: 30 m

Sail area: 692 m²

Displacement: 206.3 tonnes

Gross tonnage: 122.9 tonnes

Nett tonnage: 36.6 tonnes

Engine: Volvo Penta, 6 cylinder, 350 hp, single screw, service speed 6 knots

OUR SVANEN

Name: OUR SVANEN
Built: Frederikssund, Denmark, 1922
Flag: British / Stornoway,
    but transferred to Canada / Vancouver at Mauritius
Signal letters: GUTM
Rig: barquentine, short-rigged
Length overall: 39.6 m

Beam: 6.7 m
Draught: 3.0 m
Mast height: 23.2 m
Sail area: 502 m²
Displacement: 355.6 tonnes
Gross tonnage: 121 tonnes
Nett tonnage: 82 tonnes

Engine: Caterpillar 3406, 6 cylinder, 350 hp,
    single screw, service speed 6 knots

THE SHIPS

BOUNTY

Name: BOUNTY
Built: Whangarei Engineering Company,
Whangarei, New Zealand, 1979
Flag: British / London
Signal letters: GIFT
Rig: 18th century flush-decked barque
Length overall: 40.5 m
Beam: 8.5 m
Draught: 3.8 m
Mast height: 29 m
Sail area: 650 m²
Displacement: 393.2 tonnes
Gross tonnage: 251.4 tonnes
Nett tonnage: 170.9 tonnes
Engine: 2 Kelvin 8 cylinder turbos, 415 hp,
twin screw, service speed 7 knots

EYE OF THE WIND

Name: EYE OF THE WIND
Flag: British / Faversham
Signal letters: GWAK
Rig: hermaphrodite brig
Length overall: 40.2 m
Beam: 7 m
Draught: 2.7 m
Mast height: 27.7 m
Sail area: 743 m²
Displacement: 264 tonnes
Gross tonnage: 152 tonnes
Nett tonnage: 116.8 tonnes
Engine: 8L3B Gardner diesel, 230 hp,
single screw, service speed 6 knots

KASKELOT

Name: KASKELOT
Built: Ring Andersen, Svendborg, Denmark, 1948
Flag: British/Jersey
Signal letters: GDQK
Rig: 19th century barque
Length overall: 46.6 m
Beam: 8.5 m
Draught: 3.7 m
Mast height: 31.4 m
Sail area: 882 m²
Displacement: 457 tonnes
Gross tonnage: 229 tonnes
Nett tonnage: 147.4 tonnes
Engine: B & W Alpha, 400 hp, single screw, service speed 7 knots

PERMANENT CREW

Tommi Nielsen (Denmark)	Master
Rob Morton (NZ)	Mate
David Raine (UK)	Second mate
David McQueen (UK)	Engineer
Dan Stinson (Australia)	Boatswain
Sam Dean (UK)	AB
Alan Dunbell (UK)	AB
Dominique Wills (UK)	AB
Caroline Eltringham (UK)	Deckhand
Jochem Howell (UK)	Deckhand
Andrea Oliver (USA)	Deckhand
Sarah White (UK)	Cook

The British barque, *Kaskelot*, sailed only from London to the departure from Portsmouth, but during that vital 28 day period she became a nucleus for the assembling First Fleet and the attendant publicity. Other commitments prevented her from sailing with the Fleet.

Kaskelot is Danish for sperm whale, and it was under this name she was built by Ring Andersen at Svendborg in Denmark in 1948, but as a wooden ketch-rigged motor vessel. Her hull is oak-on-beech on oaken frames, the whole strengthened for ice work, and she was the largest wooden vessel built anywhere in the world since 1880. She first traded to the Danish dependency of Greenland for the Royal Greenland Trading Company, serving the small coastal settlements below the Arctic Circle as both cargo and hospital ship. Later she worked cargoes around another Danish dependency, the Faroe Islands in the Atlantic Ocean north of Scotland, under a variety of names.

But, with the world decline in shipping in the 1970s, she had progressively fewer and fewer cargoes until she was eventually laid-up in Denmark. When her present owners, Square Sail of Britain, found her in 1983 she had virtually become a derelict. Her second lease of life began near Svendborg, where her hull was restored, massive oaken deck frames fitted, her decks relaid and three masts of Douglas Fir stepped. She was rigged as a barque — her yards and spars also of Douglas Fir — with deadeyes of traditional greenheart, a close grained hardwood used in sailing ships of old. And she was restored to her original name.

Kaskelot's first charter with Square Sail was in the television series about the struggle to achieve the South Pole, "The Last Place On Earth", in which she sailed to Norway, Scotland and Greenland as Scott's *Terra Nova* and Amundsen's *Fram*. Further television work followed and then a charter for the film *Revolution* about the American Wars of Independence. At the time of the First Fleet expedition, *Kaskelot* was filming in *Return To Treasure Island*.

LONDON TO PORTSMOUTH

27 April to 30 April 1987

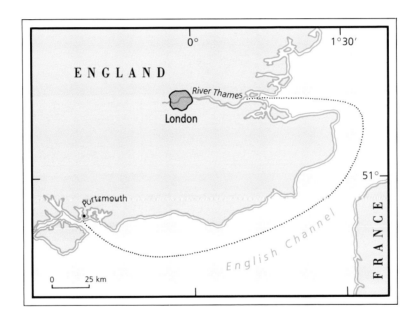

Amorina, largest of the First Fleet Re-enactment ships, glides gracefully between
the massive stone towers of Tower Bridge after slipping her moorings at Tower Pier.
Behind her, the dome of St Pauls commands the London skyline as it did when the
original Fleet sailed from there in 1787.

Far left: The flagship, the *Soren Larsen*, leads the Fleet down the Thames to the sea. The gaskets on the three upper yards have been cast off, and the crew prepare more sail in the unusually light April winds. **Above:** *Amorina* tacks across the river under sail and motors to avoid some of the small craft. **Left:** Jonathan King, descendant of Lieutenant Philip Gidley King RN who served on the 1787 flagship HMS *Sirius*, poses on the jib boom of the 1987 flagship.

Above: In line astern *Soren Larsen*, *R. Tucker Thompson* (foreground) and *Tradewind* drop down the river to the sea. London's Docklands — witness to many other historic sailings through the centuries — are now being refurbished in a new lease of life.   **Right:** *Tucker Thompson* (the "R" was soon dropped from her name by the rest of the Fleet and later her name abbreviated even further to *Tucker T.*) gathers speed as her fore and aft sails catch the breeze. That night the Fleet anchored in thick fog opposite Southend, but the following morning was able to weigh anchor and proceed outward past the South Foreland.

PORTSMOUTH TO TENERIFE

13 May to 29 May 1987

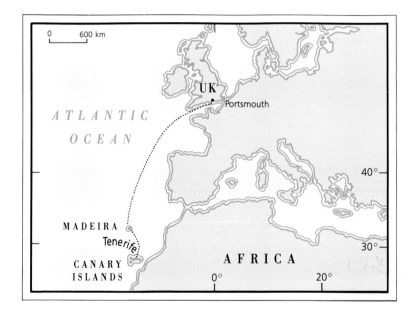

Our Svanen is moored alongside *Bounty* at the battleship berth at HM Naval
Dockyard, Portsmouth.

Above: *Bounty* flies the Red Duster at her ensign staff, while the old naval ensign that the original vessel flew in 1787 is flown at her jack. The historical coincidences in 1987 were numerous. Captain Bligh left from Portsmouth for the South Seas on HMS *Bounty* in 1787, only months after the First Fleet sailed — Bligh and Phillip were in port together and had originally planned to sail together as far as Rio de Janeiro. Two hundred years later *Bounty* berthed in Portsmouth once again, only 100 metres from Nelson's flagship at Trafalgar, HMS *Victory.*   **Right:** Work continues on the *Soren Larsen* to prepare for sailing on 12 May to the Motherbank off Ryde, Isle of Wight, where the original Fleet anchored before leaving England. Note the "cock-billed" course yard which is dipped to give space for the vessel alongside (*Kaskelot*).   **Opposite page:** *R. Tucker Thompson* swings out into the stream on 12 May while the crew on *Bounty* are still bending on the spritsail to its yard beneath the bowsprit.

From the starboard bridge wing of the present HMS *Sirius,* HM the Queen and HRH Prince Philip review the First Fleet anchored on the Motherbank. On Her Majesty's left, the Queen's Harbour Master for Portsmouth, Captain Chamberlen, explains a point of interest while Sir Peter Gadsden, Chairman of the Britain–Australia Bicentennial Committee, looks on. In honour of the original flagship, the First Fleet Re-enactment command pennant is the yellow Sirius star — brightest star in the heavens — on a blue background.
Below: *Bounty* waits to proceed seawards. In 1787 HMS *Sirius* gave the signal to the First Fleet to weigh anchor and proceed to sea, and on 13 May 1987 another *Sirius* repeats that order to the Re-enactment Fleet by lowering the signal UWRV1 in the International Code: "I wish you a pleasant voyage. You should proceed to your destination." But the clement spring weather is at an end, and a gale is forecast for the afternoon and night of 13 May. **Opposite page, above:** Sailing down the Solent. From left to right: *Johanna Lucretia, Royalist, R. Tucker Thompson, Amorina, Anna Kristina, Tradewind, Lord Nelson, Our Svanen, Kaskelot. Johanna Lucretia, Royalist, Lord Nelson* and *Kaskelot* sailed with the Fleet out of the Solent to bring the number to the original eleven.

Right: Because of a minor breakdown on the flagship, the vice-flagship *Bounty* leads the ships away from the Motherbank while urgent repairs are carried out on the *Soren Larsen* with equipment lent by the QHM, Captain Chamberlen. **Far right:** A last farewell from England in Solent water. The wind and sea begin to rise and a lowering sky sweeps in from the west.

The expected sou'westerly blow came up the Channel from the Atlantic and the Fleet spent its first night of the passage to Tenerife sheltering in the lee of the Isle of Wight in St Helens Roads; if they had attempted to beat down Channel many ships would have ended up back near Dover. The following afternoon the gale abated and the Fleet sailed from St Helens Roads, around the south of the Isle of Wight and down the Channel for Ushant and the Western Approaches. So many ships, convoys and fleets have sailed these same waters from Great Britain; the last land the First Fleet sighted was the Lizard, the most southerly point of these misty islands.

Above right: "Haul boys!" and the heavy yards on the *Soren Larsen* are braced around to starboard. It is all manpower on these traditional sailing ships, and while one man hauls out and down to the belaying pin a second man "tails" and reeves in the slack.   **Above left:** On *Amorina*, in the Atlantic, the crew prepare the mainsail for hoisting after some minor repairs have been completed. But there are always moments of relaxation. The safety net at the bow is a favourite spot for stretching out, and Tony Curtis, experienced seaman as well as cameraman in the documentary team, reflects upon square-rig sailing.

Out of the Channel and steering south, the weather improved again. Dolphins are harbingers of good weather, and in apparent delight they leap and frolic around the bows of all types of vessels — but it can be a dangerous sport. Pointing downwards from the bowsprit is a length of timber or steel called the dolphin striker, used to give purchase to and to tension the bobstay. As the ship dips into the ocean swell the dolphin striker also dips down sometimes into the water, and on the *Soren Larsen* (above) this happened just as a dolphin curved across the bow. The wooden dolphin striker actually struck the poor mammal — surely a million to one chance — and in the next instant all the dolphins had swum away.

Right: *Soren Larsen* and *Bounty* in company running free towards Tenerife. *Bounty*'s main course is handed to allow the wind to blow through to her fore square-sails, a traditional arrangement in square-rig sailing to prevent blanketing the sails. It is often preferred to set the fore as opposed to the main course because the fore gives lift to the bow.

Far left: Aftermath of the gales in the North Atlantic; the bobstay eye around the base of the dolphin striker has sheered after constant pounding into the sea. Sitting on the chains is third mate and shipwright David "Croc" Mitchell. **Left:** This long-fin tuna can count himself unlucky to be hooked — the delight at this rare catch shows on David's face. **Above:** Clare Puntis and Duncan Reed won their places on the First Fleet Re-enactment through Portsmouth City Council in Hampshire. Portsmouth and Sydney are sister cities.

Above: Ready for the oven, this tray of Red Schnapper should satisfy the healthy appetite of most crews. The style of cooking varies from ship to ship and from cook to cook — whether it is roasted chicken or a Chinese dish the cook's job is as demanding as any on board. Deputy Surgeon Peter Riddel (left) diverts his cutting talents to gut fish for *Amorina's* cook, Susan Hall. Trainee John Ellicott waits to eat the result.   **Right:** The wind rises again during the passage across the Atlantic, and the hands turn to haul a second reef in the main. It is always tempting to leave the sails set and keep the vessel flying along, but when the ship is over-pressed the strain on the gear aloft is phenomenal and the ship becomes very difficult to steer; *"Any fool can carry on but only the wise man knows how to shorten sail in time."* — Joseph Conrad, June 1923.

In 1787 the First Fleet anchored out in the bay off Santa Cruz de Tenerife, but this First Fleet berthed alongside in the new harbour by the centre of town.   **Right:** *Amorina* glides gently into the basin under her "iron topsail" on 29 May after sailing 2700 kilometres since Portsmouth. The crew out on the footropes on the lower topsail yard are harbour-stowing the sail. This involves loosening the sheets and bunts, rolling the sail into itself and lifting in onto the top forepart of the yard, as has already been done on the course, upper topsail and topgallant.

Above: First Fleet office, Tenerife. No desk or revolving padded chair or air conditioning for this executive — but at least the telephone has not been vandalised!

The first changeover of trainee crew took place in Tenerife, the Fleet's first major port of call, in early June. Traditional Canary Island folk dancing and singing on the quay farewelled the ships, and on a blustery but sunny day the seven small ships left harbour. The eighth ship, *One and All,* was transiting the Suez Canal, hoping to catch the Fleet in the Atlantic.

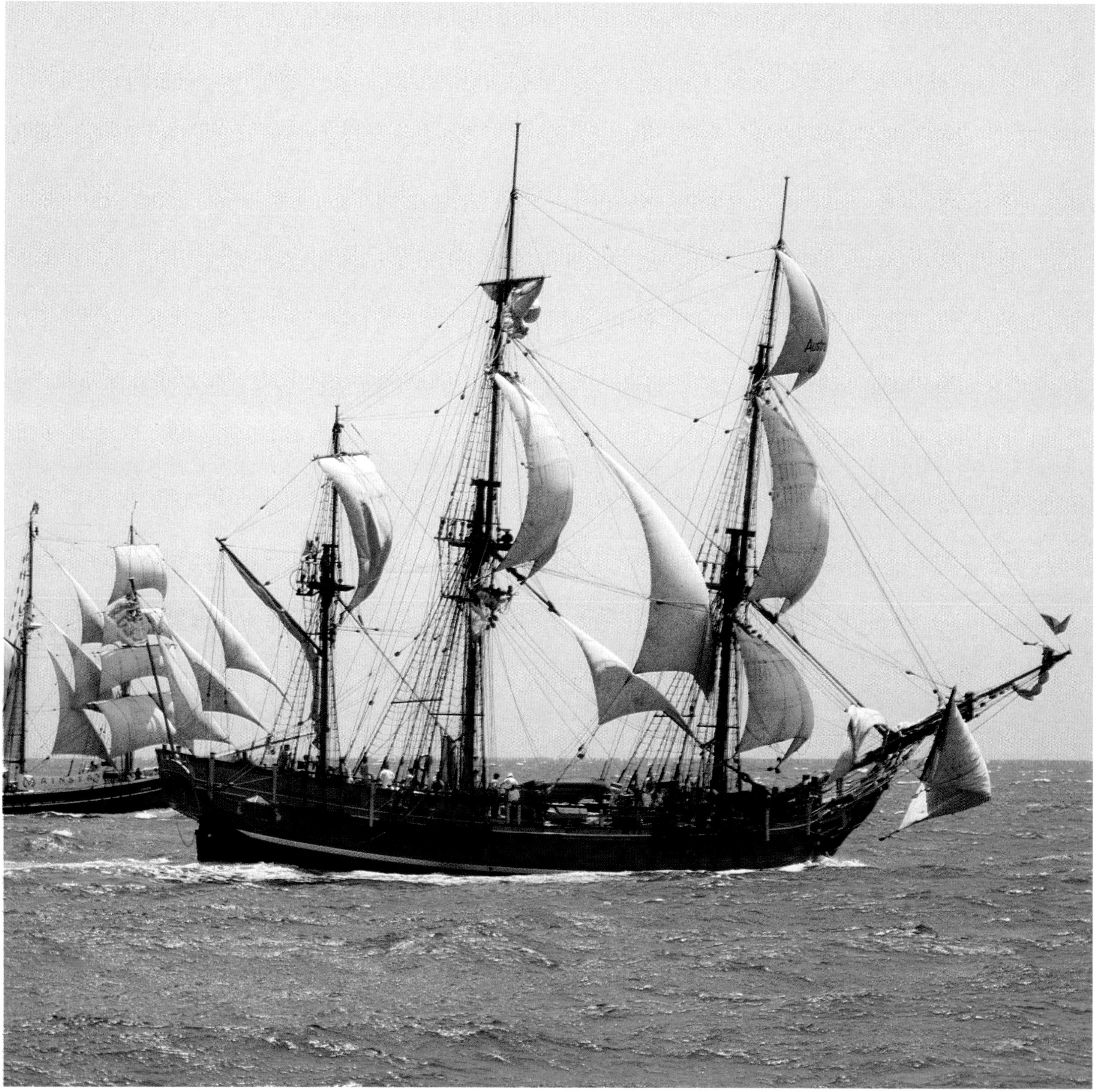

TENERIFE TO RIO DE JANEIRO

9 June to 26 July 1987

In perfect sailing weather *Our Svanen* and *Bounty* thrash out to sea in a stiff breeze
from Santa Cruz and head southwards to the tropics.

After casting-off from the quay, the heavy mooring ropes are coiled, dried and stowed below decks in the rope locker.
Right: From left to right, *Amorina*'s Second Mate Peter Breid, Third Mate Ziggie Gustafsson and trainee Jack Mortimer clear the decks in their "*Amorina* uniforms". The other ships soon followed suit, each with their own dress uniform for port arrivals and departures. **Above:** Five squares set–fore course, lower topsail, upper topsail, t'gallant and the royal — a view from the mizzen main-top on the barquentine *Amorina*. **Opposite page:** "Shooting" the sun with the marine sextant gives Bosun Dan Stinson a position line along which the ship is — somewhere. Running this fix forward (usually the noon fix when the ship's latitude is found) gives the ship's latitude and longitude, at the point where the two position lines cross. The ships also use electronic satellite fixes, but a check of these is always made by traditional celestial navigation with the sextant.

Glorious days in the tropics. Bowling along in the trade winds is surely one of the greatest experiences in sail, and to make such a passage on a square-rigger in the company of other square-riggers is icing on the cake. **Above:** Brigantine *Soren Larsen* in the sights of trainee Charlotte Thamo on board barquentine *Amorina* in the northeast trades. **Bottom:** During the day, lectures and instruction on navigation, ropework, sail-trimming and other ancient mariners' arts are given on all ships; you might learn to shoot the sun, tie a Matthew Walker or Turk's Head, or how to fan the yards. They will not turn a landsman into a seaman overnight, but they are a beginning, and many trainees continue sailing afterwards as a result of their experiences. Others, of course, swear never to set foot on a deck again.

But when the wind dies and the sun shines, it is into the sea to cool off and swim. The sails are handed to stop them flapping and chafing in their gear, a shark watch posted aloft, and then follows a welcome dip in the ocean alongside the gently rolling ship.

An unscheduled stop in Mindelo, Sao Vincente, an old Royal Naval coaling and oiling port in the Cape Verde Islands, gave a welcome break in the long voyage to Rio. The galeas *Anna Kristina* had broken her main gaff two nights before, but was able to use a local shipyard to fit a steel "sleeve" over the break.

Above: Porto Grande, with the Fleet anchored close in to shelter from the strong katebatic wind that roared off the mountains. From left to right: *Bounty, Our Svanen, R. Tucker Thompson, Soren Larsen, Tradewind, Anna Kristina,* and *Amorina.* **Right:** Children followed photographer Malcolm Clarke through the streets of Mindelo until he finally agreed to photograph them — then, all smiles.

Above left: Street-sellers with their wares. The ships replenished their fruit and vegetable supplies with local produce, a luxury the First Fleet had been denied 200 years before as they sailed past the Cape Verde Islands. The local economy boomed during the Re-enactment Fleet's 3 day invasion, but severe bouts of dysentery laid low many of the crews a few days later. **Above right:** In the back streets.

Bottom: Refreshed after leave ashore, the crews set sail again for the run to Brazil. At a masters' meeting in Mindelo it was decided to make a landfall at Bahia de Salvador, just south of the mouth of the Amazon, and in a spanking nor'easterly force 5 the ships left the Cape Verde Islands. Left to right: *Our Svanen, Tradewind*, and *Soren Larsen* passing south down the Ile de St Antâo.

In the Doldrums: In the area across the equator between the northern hemisphere northeast trade wind and the southern hemisphere southeast trades lies a belt of little and variable winds, the scourge of sailing ships for centuries. These latitudes are called the doldrums and square-riggers have spent weeks crossing them, though at other times some have kept sailing straight through in a shaft of wind in a few days. The Re-enactment Fleet had no such luck and so the sails were handed, the motors engaged, and it was gin and tonic on the afterdeck. As the ships sailed from east to west across the International Time Zone, clocks were put back: the longer sunsets were fabulous.

Opposite page: Still on her maiden voyage, the Australian jackass brigantine *One and All* was sailing for Gibraltar for repairs to her topmast. Some of the Oregon was weak, and this problem would delay her rendezvous with the Fleet by about six days. Captain Colin Kesteven, who also skippered the *Bounty* from Vancouver to Australia, can only muse on the likely date of his first sighting of the Fleet.

But south of the equator southeast trades begin to set in, and it's rolling down to Rio.

Opposite page: *Soren Larsen* lifts her wings and begins to fly across the ocean. With the wind on her port quarter two of her headsails — the inner jib and the fore-top mast staysail — are in their gaskets. These headsails are blanketed by the squares and so would only flog and chafe if they were hoisted. The outer jib is set in case the vessel accidentally rounds up to the wind, and it will then draw properly and help turn the vessel back down wind again.

Top: A transfer at sea, always a difficult operation in a heavy swell. With Henrik lost and another crew member with an ankle broken during the emergency, *Anna Kristina*'s crew are stretched to the limit, so the flagship transferred the Fleet Surgeon Rob Simpson, and Norwegian-speaking Bosun John Gryska, to help share the load.

Bottom: *Our Svanen* drives across the South Atlantic in the vanguard of the Fleet. Even with her mainsail handed — the jaws of the gaff boom parted and the spar was sent down to be repaired on deck — and the topgallant and mizzen-gaff topsail handed, the old wooden ship still flies in a steady breeze. The lines trailing aft are her emergency steering chains, connected to the rudder outside the hull in case the internal gearing fails.

Above: The crew on *Amorina* stand by for the order to haul away, while others take off the gaskets from around the mainsail **(bottom left)**. But for Gordon Carvosso **(bottom right)** it all becomes too much. While the world sails by, he lies oblivious in the sun. Apart from a break between Mauritius and Fremantle, Gordon sailed all the way from London to Sydney.

Above: Apart from needing a good head for heights — it is often difficult to find a firm foothold against which to brace, as exemplified by trainee Fred Pentecost. **Bottom:** In crowded conditions at sea one learns to love and hate, and to hide both emotions. But when affection is returned, love blossoms. Two engagements were announced during the voyage. **Far left:** *Our Svanen* alongside *Amorina* — in calm seas the ships sometimes came within a few yards of each other to exchange gifts and news. Trainee John Lind is unperturbed.

Above: Setting sail from Salvador for the coastal passage south to Rio. Modern Salvador dominates the old quarter, but this port was the first European settlement in Brazil and was the former capital of the old Portuguese colony. **Below:** Meeting the first ocean swells at the entrance to Bahia, left to right: *Anna Kristina,* with her distinctive ochre-brown sails, *Tradewind* avoiding a yacht, *Our Svanen,* with her boats still in their davits — red boat for port, green for starboard — and *R. Tucker Thompson* heeling to a gust. All vessels still sailing under fore-aft sails only — the squares are set outside the bay.

We made our South American landfall at Bahia de Salvador, 1368 kilometres north of Rio de Janeiro and just south of the southern headland of the Amazon estuary. The women of Bahia wear calf-length, white brocaded cotton dresses with red bandanas and scarves, flashing gold earrings and soft brown leather boots. In the markets they sit and hand-roll the famous Salvador cigars, and as they walk down the verandahed streets in the old quarter they swing their hips and their skirts sway against their legs. We got into trouble in Salvador. The Fleet anchored off the exclusive yacht club (**above**) and, as sailors will, the crews went ashore and drank, and fell into the swimming pool and, being mixed crew, kissed and frolicked and the following day were banned from the club. On Ipanema and Copacabana in sophisticated Rio the girls wear tiny string bikinis, but north in Bahia it's different. We soon learnt.

Right: The island of Santa Barbara, on the way south from Salvador, a nature reserve where the caretakers/naturalists live with their families for a two year contract. The crew of *Amorina* were taken over the reserve when they anchored off for the day.

SAILING HOME

At last! Rio de Janeiro — January River — a major port for over 400 years. This is where the First Fleet and Captain Bligh stopped on their voyages south in 1787, and where, until the arrival of the First Fleet Re-enactment in 1987, Australia was the country most people had never heard of. The welcome was stupendous, and a major media event throughout Brazil.

Top right: *Bounty* sails beneath the giant statue of Jesus Christ on Corcovado, part of the parade of sail that took square-rigged ships past Copacabana, Ipanema and Leblon beaches and back, before entering Rio harbour in line behind the flagship. From Corcovado, Rio is laid out below like a relief map, and the extent of one of the biggest natural harbours in the world can be fully seen. **Below:** The wind failed the Fleet, on Sunday 26 July, and the sails hung limply as the ships were forced to use their motors to enter past Sugarloaf and berth at the passenger terminal. From London the First Fleet had sailed 9932 nautical miles. Rio was half-way port to Sydney, but despite the incredible welcome and enthusiasm here, in Australia trouble was looming.

A forest of masts, spars, and quayside derricks, and a seemingly unending vista of rigging — *Bounty* alone carries over 17 kilometres of rigging. Much of the maintenance and many of the repairs can only be completed in port, so for the crews it is still day watches and night ship-keeps as the work continues. In port, all the time is spent in getting the ship ready for sea, while the time at sea is spent clearing her up after the last port and preparing her for the next.

Above: In Rio, one of many ship's meetings to discuss the financial crisis. **Bottom left:** Mike Kichenside, with Maurine Goldston-Morris of Sydney, presents the Australian Heritage flag to Antonio Luis Porto E Alburquerque of the Natural History Museum.
Bottom right: Lieutenant Armando Repinaldo (left) of the Brazilian Navy with David Iggulden (right) and Gerry Weingarth.

On Corcovado, a giant statue of Jesus Christ appears to offer succour to all in need, but (**above**) First Fleet Re-enactment founder Dr Jonathan King ponders on the possibility of half the ships turning back through lack of funds. **Bottom:** Even Great Train Robber Ronald Biggs supports the Fleet, but feels some homesickness as the ships prepare to leave Brazil, for he is doomed by his own actions to stay forever or risk jail in Britain.

RIO DE JANEIRO
TO
CAPE TOWN

9 August to 10 September 1987

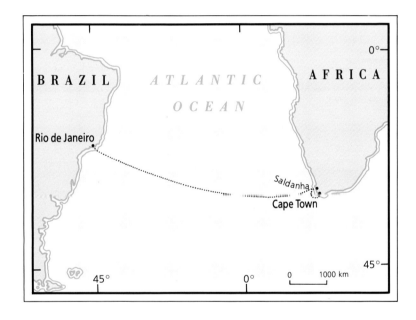

Flagship *Soren Larsen* leads the Fleet outward bound from Rio on Sunday 9 August
1987 heading for Cape Town.

The Fleet anchored at Cabo Buzios, 100 kilometres north of Rio, to paint and scrape the ships.

Above: *Tradewind* tries some new flag hoists. **Right:** This unflattering stern view of *Amorina* shows the saloon that was added to her poop during the conversion in Portugal in 1980-83. **Far right:** A liberty boat returns to *Bounty* from the shore. **Opposite page:** *Bounty* motor-sailing in light winds.

After the Fleet left Rio, *One and All* at last caught up. The ships rendezvoused, and *One and All* entered Rio for water and supplies before following on. The weather was kind at first — Force 3 winds and slight seas — and the mood was relaxed after the rigours of Rio. People caught up on their diaries, took to hammocks or even the deck.

Above: When there is little happening, there is little to film, so Tony Curtis takes a break from the documentary and ship's watches. Despite the sunshine and shadows, the heavy clothing tells another story about the weather.   **Right:** This would never have happened in Captain Arthur Phillip's day. All ships use a system of watches at sea, but some vary in detail. *Our Svanen* and *Bounty* have a two watch system — watch on, watch off; *Soren Larsen, Amorina,* and *One and All* have a 4 hour on, 8 hour off three watch system; *R. Tucker Thompson* and *Anna Kristina* use a Scandinavian system which continually rotates the watches throughout the day.   **Opposite page, bottom right:** Tristan Davies, 7, rushes forward to find out if there is still "nothing happening" on the *Soren Larsen*. Tristan and sister Natasha, 4, children of skipper Tony and wife Fleur Davies, sailed all the way from London to Sydney.

The weather deteriorated and by the middle of August the small ships were beset by gales. **Opposite page:** *Anna Kristina* under shortened sail. **Above:** *Soren Larsen*, with deadlights protecting her wheelhouse windows, dips her leeward rail under. **Bottom left:** "Dinty" Moore risks a soaking as he takes vegetables from a deck locker. **Bottom right:** Trainee Stephen Mundell tries to keep his feet.

Keeping a sharp look out for alien objects or other ships is one of the most important "activities".
Above: Roelof Brouwen at the bow during his early morning watch.
Bottom Left: Tony Davies, captain of *Soren Larsen,* and Commodore Mike Kichenside scan the horizon. Sometimes, as when searching for lost seaman Henrik Nielsen, watches are interspersed equally around the decks **(bottom right).**

Far left: Looking like an ancient Viking invader scanning the horizon for new lands to conquer, Anne von Bertouch — who was sailing with the Fleet from London to Sydney. **Above:** Trainee Peter Ellicott (foreground) looks forlornly out to sea in the desperate hope that he might see some sign of the *Anna Kristina*'s First Mate. **Bottom:** Tension and sadness are portrayed on the face of the oldest trainee, 74-year-old Wendy Newton, as she realises that the chances of survival in such a hostile environment are very slim.

The worst done, the weather relents and the quarterdeck resumes its role as lying down deck (**bottom**). **Above:** *R. Tucker Thompson* as seen from the deck of *Soren Larsen*. **Far left:** A bird's-eye view of *Soren Larsen*.

Knots, bends, turns, splices and all things ropey and nautical, bearing in mind that there are only ever two ropes on board a vessel — the bell rope and the bucket rope. Everything else is a line, or a sheet, or a pennant, or a halyard, or a lift, or a brace, or a tack, or. . .

Below: First Mate Dan Yates (right) gives lessons in the ancient sailors' art to trainee crew in an age group spanning 50 years. **Above:** The Rio to Cape Town passage is almost over as the flagship motors along the tip of Southern Africa into Table Bay and the old port of Cape Town. The wind decreases to a light sou'easterly for the morning arrival of 10 September, and several of the ships, especially the wooden-hulled vessels, experience magnetic anomalies to their steering compasses in the southern Cape Province waters.

Above: The lovely *Anna Kristina* comes alongside after her traumatic 32 day passage across the South Atlantic. The following day a simple service was held for Henrik Nielsen in St Martin's Lutheran Church in the city, at which the whole Fleet attended. A message from Henrik's family was read to the crews.

Below: With the stunning backdrop of Table Mountain, the eight vessels of the First Fleet Re-enactment voyage lie in port together for the first time. The Australian *One and All* is third from left, easily recognisable by her beautiful, low, schooner-style transom.

Captain Phillip met with resistance and unfriendliness here in 1787 — the Dutch-controlled settlement was suspicious of the intentions of the British — but 200 years later the welcome could not have been friendlier.

Below: The costume welcome on the quayside at Duncan Dock is one that Phillip would have recognised had he ever received one. The band played, the banners streamed, the children shouted, and the girls smiled; the port was a rainbow of colour and cheering crowds. **Above:** The Mayor of Cape Town, Peter Muller, officially welcomed the Fleet and with the Town Clerk escorted Commodore Mike Kichenside on a tour of the city in the Mayoral coach — an open landau — with the other masters following in other coaches.

But, as in every port, repair and maintenance take precedence, and slipping the vessels for hull inspection and antifouling is a priority. **Above:** On *Tradewind*, Captain Mark Hammond fits a new section to the straight up-and-down bow, giving her more flowing lines. **Left:** The antifouling is rolled onto *Tradewind*'s bottom, while (**bottom**) the topsides of *Soren Larsen* receive a final coat. **Opposite page:** The barquentine *Our Svanen* leading *Tradewind* in the parade of sail before Table Mountain at Cape Town.

CAPE TOWN TO MAURITIUS

28 September to 29 October 1987

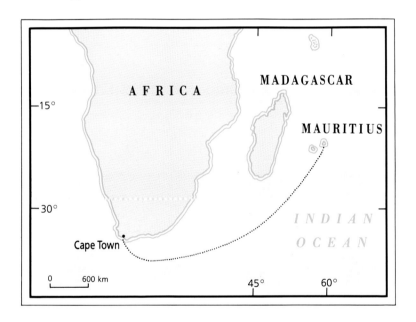

Too soon it's time to put to sea again. 26 January 1988 in Australia is suddenly
much closer, and with new complements of trainee crews
the Fleet departs Cape Town.

Bottom left: *Soren Larsen* slips out into Table Bay with (**bottom right**) *Our Svanen* and *Tradewind* in close attendance — plus an uncomfortably close media helicopter.
Above: *Bounty* is the last to leave Duncan Dock. There is a distinct absence of wind in Cape Town this 28th day of September.

Out in Table Bay and southward to the Cape of Good Hope, or Cape of Storms, the wind continues light and variable, but the Fleet makes an impressive spectacle of sail as they move slowly south into the Southern Ocean. **Above:** From left to right, the gaff-rigged square-topsailed schooner, *R. Tucker Thompson*, the galeas *Anna Kristina*, the barquentine *Our Svanen*, the gaff-rigged square-topsailed schooner *Tradewind*, and the barquentine *Amorina*. The Fleet sailed southwards rather than eastwards towards Mauritius to avoid the extremely dangerous Agulhas Bank, and the Agulhas currents which flow onto the Bank along the eastern coast of South Africa. Dangerous breaking seas and "abnormal waves" are prevalent in these waters. **Bottom:** Another view of part of the Fleet with Table Mountain and the Lion's Head behind.

Above: Four of the largest ships in company: *Amorina,* in the foreground with, left to right, the hermaphrodite brigantine *One and All, Bounty,* and *Soren Larsen,* outward-bound from Cape Town.

Bottom: Motor-sailing almost dead into the light winds to clear Table Bay. In the olden days these vessels would have had to wait for a fairer wind or spend a day or more beating slowly out to sea. The original First Fleet was blown several hundred kilometres back into the Atlantic before they were finally able to begin heading eastwards towards Australia.

Opposite page: A stunning aerial photograph of *Soren Larsen* flying the Australian Heritage flag at her jack. The Lion's Head is showing clearly behind her headsails.

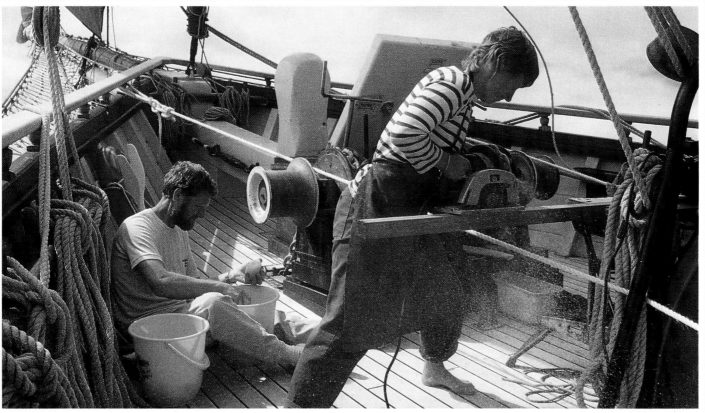

The *One and All* brought a new, distinctly Australian flavour to the multi-national First Fleet, and the dry Aussie humour was a welcome addition to the four radio schedules each day. **Above:** On the foredeck in fine weather shipwright Noni Howard is busy with her circular saw while trainee Michael Keats determinedly prepares lunch. A role reversal in some eyes, but at sea everyone from the Master down begins their training by polishing the brightwork and peeling the spuds. The next stage is sanding, scraping and painting, but on small sailing ships like these of the First Fleet Re-enactment even the Bosun turns to the more mundane tasks. Ship care is never ending, a continuous cycle of maintenance, repair, replacement, refurbishment and improvement to keep the vessel in survey and seaworthy.

Someone on a ship always becomes the barber. Here it is nurse and deckhand Stephanie Calderwood giving piratical looking Master, Colin Kesteven, a much needed trim. **Above:** Mike Hanson takes a Fleet radio sched at night in the navigation room of *One and All*. Each ship reports its position, course and speed as well as other information every six hours. **Bottom:** Engineer Neil Wigan comes up from his "pit" to survey the real world of natural light and air, and to clear his lungs with a fresh pipe.

The weather deteriorates the further the ships are from Africa, and the sea and swell build up from the south. *R. Tucker Thompson* and *Soren Larsen* manoeuvre for film work in the Fleet television documentary while reaching on the port tack, now in the Southern Indian Ocean. *Soren's* main is handed at this stage to slow her down for *R. Tucker Thompson*, *Iradewind* and *Anna Kristina* to close on her.

Right: Able seaman Kevin Priestly keeps an eye on trainee Tracy Rowan at the helm of *One and All*. The sun is still shining, but note the swell building up behind and the wet weather gear the watch is wearing.

Far Left: Penny Oxenbridge on the fore-topmast shrouds is one who hopes to find a full-time career at sea after the expedition. Out on the yard (**above**) requires good balance, a head for heights, and a strong arm to hold on. Although you stand on the footrope, this should only be used for balance — the body weight should be on top of the yard, through the stomach. But it's easier said than done. **Bottom:** The hoop around the wheel prevents the main sheets and reefing pennants from catching in the otherwise open spokes.

The decks are sometimes dry (**above left**) and sometimes wet.

Above right: Trainee Mark Leach gets a dowsing as a swell sweeps across the deck.

Bottom: It is drier at the wheel but wet weather gear is still the order of the day for going on deck. The ball by the compass is positioned to counteract deviation — the magnetic effect on the compass caused by metal in the ship's structures. There are two, one either side of the compass, and they have been the subject of many a ribald joke with their name of Compensating Balls.

Opposite page: In lighter winds approaching Mauritius, a beautiful shot of *R. Tucker Thompson* as she prepares to set a water-sail beneath her boom. When running before the wind on a port jibe, the idea is to harness the wind passing underneath the mainsail to give the ship more drive. *R. Tucker Thompson* is a well sponsored vessel.

On the exotic Indian Ocean island of Mauritius, an International Festival of the Sea has been organised around the arrival of the First Fleet Re-enactment ships, the largest fleet of sail to berth at Mauritius since the Napoleonic Wars. Australia Week brought the Fleet as the greatest attraction of the entire Festival, surpassing the British, French, and American Weeks. With the carnival atmosphere in the capital, Port Louis, various crews went shopping to improve their ship's "uniform" for their arrival in Australia.

Above: On *R. Tucker Thompson* they chose shirts and a variety of hats as the basis for their ship's garb. From left to right: Kim, Melanie, Russell, Greta and Tod.

Bottom: Those of the *One and All* opted for exotic shorts — long — for their ship's trademark. From left to right: "Sly", Don, Dick, Tracy, Mike and Charlotte.

Right: Other crews preferred a casual, non-identifiable celebration of local fashion, with just straw hats and come-as-you-are smiles. From left to right and top to bottom: John, Artie, Miranda, Dan, Pete and Gary.

Above: While in port, alfresco dining on deck becomes popular. Without the movements of the vessel through the water there is little or no air movement below deck, and during the day, especially, it becomes stifling and humid in the tropics. Local produce vies with fresh ship's stores at the table — Kerry and Tony wait for the dinner bell.

MAURITIUS TO FREMANTLE

10 November to 12 December 1987

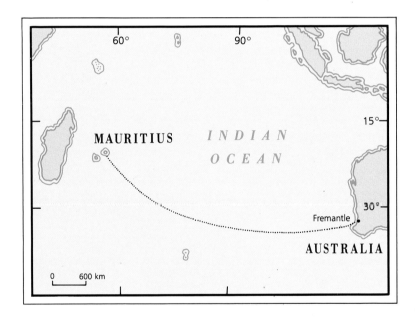

With the International Festival of the Sea completed — finishing with official receptions on the *Soren Larsen, Our Svanen* and *Bounty* and a gala ball on the wharf — the small ships return to sea on 10 November for the Indian Ocean crossing, and Australian landfall at Fremantle.

Furling square-sails on *Bounty* (**opposite page**) is hard work, using the old system of "handing" the sails. The corners, or clews, of the sail are hauled up to the yards by the clew-lines from the deck, and then the hands aloft haul the body, or bunt, of the sail up to the yard by brute strength for furling and gasketing. When sailing in the higher latitudes in winter handing the sail virtually meant hauling up a stiff board of frozen canvas — and broken and bleeding fingers and nails. Reefs are taken in the same fashion.

Later in the 19th century ships fitted many more buntlines, which enabled the whole sail to be hauled up to its yard from the deck. Work aloft became easier, and the first steps were made to reduce the size of crews as a result.

This page: Under fore and aft sails only, *Bounty* plugs across the Indian Ocean. On this leg there were few good sailing days. As before, the Fleet split into two squadrons: *Our Svanen, One and All, R. Tucker Thompson, Tradewind* and *Anna Kristina* taking the more direct northerly route following the available winds, while *Amorina, Bounty* and *Soren Larsen* followed the traditional sailing ship route to the south before turning east to catch the prevailing westerly winds. *Bounty*'s house flag — the original 1787 ensign — is drying on the leeward rail.

Then on a calm day, one of the strangest and saddest sights of the entire voyage: a great white sperm whale — like the legendary Moby Dick — floating dead on its side. Above the 12 metre mammal hundreds of sooty albatrosses and white chinned petrels wheeled and fed on the blubber and flesh; below, 3 metre long sharks circled lazily, tearing chunks out of the belly of the great whale.

Captain Adrian Small manoeuvred *Bounty* alongside, and first mate Peter Manthorpe and bosun Dan Stinson tried to retrieve the jawbone. Wearing old shoes with nails hammered through the soles the two stepped onto the young female whale's back (**above**) and attached lines to the jaws. They then began to saw through the tough bone, but with sharks continually attacking the carcass one slip may have been their last, and they eventually clambered back aboard ship. Thirty-two teeth were counted.

The cause of death of this rare mammal while still young is not certain, but it appeared that part of the rear of the whale had been blown off.

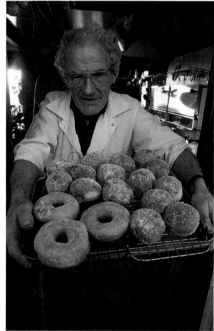

Far left: Just a few of the 17 kilometres of rope that make up *Bounty*'s standing and running rigging. The two posts supporting the bowsprit are the knightheads. These are the famous "heads" of a vessel, and on the beakhead area at the foot of the knightheads is the original seamen's latrine. **Above:** A steady deck and a barbecue while, **left**, baker "Dinty" Moore produces some of his famous doughnuts — some filled with jam and some with apple, unheard of luxuries 200 years ago.

The two "grand old sailors" of the Fleet.
Above: Commodore Mike Kichenside finally brought to his knees! The wire "azimuth ring" atop the steering compass on the flagship casts a shadow across the compass card, giving the sun's bearing according to this compass, at this GMT, at this latitude and longitude. When applied to special tables the true bearing of the sun can be calculated, and the difference between these two bearings gives the compass error. If the vessel is turned slowly through 360 degrees the error and deviation for all bearings can be found, and this operation is called "swinging the compass".
Below: Captain Adrian Small gives navigation and course information to trainee crew during a lecture on Bounty. Adrian served his apprenticeship in sail in one of the last post-war grain square-riggers from Australia to Britain, the famous Passat. He has also sailed under the legendary Alan Villiers, one of the early patrons of the First Fleet, and captained the Golden Hinde and the Nonsuch replicas during their re-enactment voyages. Mike began his sea-going career with P&O, and then moved into sail with the New Endeavour in Australia. He was Commodore of both the British world-wide expeditions "Operation Drake" and "Operation Raleigh", sailing in the Eye of the Wind and Sir Walter Raleigh respectively.

The *Soren Larsen,* **above**, brings the fleet through Gage Roads and into the Swan River in a stiff breeze, and is caught here just setting her upper topsail. *Anna Kristina* and *One and All* follow through the crowd of small craft that welcomed the ships to their first Australian port.

Right: From *Bounty*'s mainmast the Australian courtesy flag flies high above the choppy waters off Fremantle, but from the fore topmast. She suffered a broken fore topgallant during the passage from Mauritius in one of the rare "blows", and had to send down her fore topgallant yard. With this arrival at Fremantle, *Bounty* completes a virtual circumnavigation of the world. For a vessel described by some critics of the First Fleet as "vulnerable" she hasn't performed too badly; Vancouver to Sydney to Fremantle to Suez to Gibraltar to Portsmouth to Rio to Cape Town to Fremantle!

Like a scene from the last century, nine square-riggers lie alongside old Fremantle wharf during Christmas 1987. The addition to the Fleet is the British brig, *Eye of the Wind,* moored alongside *Tradewind,* which joined the expedition for the final passage around the south of Australia to Sydney. The wharf was thrown open to the public, and thousands came down to walk over the ships — the first Australians to be able to do so. A carnival atmosphere prevails, with a display of gifts received by the Fleet during its voyage, strolling buskers and shantymen, and even two girls playing flute and guitar.

One and All, still on her maiden voyage, also crossed her outward track off Fremantle, completing a rather wide circumnavigation of Africa! The crew of all the ships were weary, but having at last reached Australia the arrival in Sydney was now only one more month away. The attitude of the First Fleet both ashore and afloat is summed up by the banner on *Amorina's* stern.

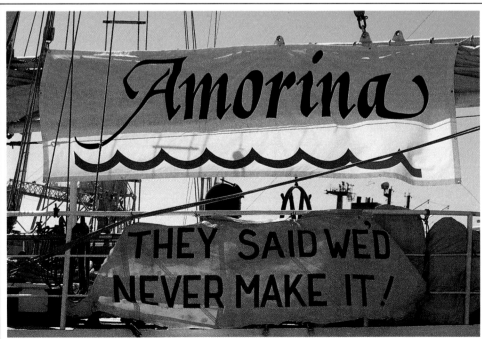

FREMANTLE TO PORT JACKSON SYDNEY
– VIA BOTANY BAY

26 December 1987 to 26 January 1988

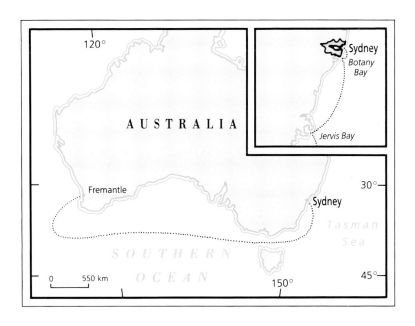

After a Christmas dinner on the wharf with the trainee crews for the last passage, the crews said goodbye to each other once again and the Fleet set sail on Boxing Day, bound for Botany Bay and Sydney. The ships were farewelled as they were welcomed, and the wharves and breakwaters were crowded with well-wishers and good luck banners.

Into the western approaches of Bass Strait between Cape Otway and King Island, and a promising front approaches the Fleet shortly after sunrise. Sails are set, **above**, as the wind makes, and the unusually placid waters begin to rise as the clouds roll through.

Above: Captain Adrian Small surveys his domain of rope, canvas, light and air from the quarter-deck of *Bounty*. In his pocket is a little something to keep away the chill. Captain Small runs his ship in the traditional manner — no talking to the helmsman when on watch. **Right:** On a brighter day, *One and All*'s golden figurehead glows in the sunlight. The bare-breasted mermaid was modelled after several of the female volunteer workers — and a centrefold pin-up — during the building of the vessel in Adelaide.

Women at sea used to be considered bad luck to ships, but times change. Captain Arthur Phillip carried over 400 female convicts in his 1787/88 Fleet of 1350 people, and the Re-enactment has carried over 350 female crew in the 1987/88 Fleet of 1000 people.

Top left: Dental surgeon Gillian Jean sets up her instruments in the *R. Tucker Thompson*'s saloon — surgery hours were generally confined to port except in emergencies of rare marine dental decay. Gillian joined the Fleet in Portsmouth on the *Amorina* and transferred her practice to many of the ships. **Top right:** Greta Thompson straps herself into the galley area on *Tucker* during a storm. The stove in this, the smallest ship of the Fleet, is set on gimbals so that whatever crazy angle she takes during rough seas the stove, pans and contents keep to the horizontal. "Fiddles" around the top of the stove prevent the pots from sliding off.

Bottom: Nurse Stephanie Calderwood relaxes for'ard on the *One and All* playing her penny whistle during a quiet evening at sea. On the Australian *One and All,* five of the ten permanent deckhands were women. **Opposite page, left:** Nurse Judi Lincoln sorts the letters and postcards sent to the Fleet from children around the world. The number received grew to such an extent that Judi became children's education contact for all the ships; talks and school visits will follow in Australia, and perhaps a book.

Above: Fleet Purser and ex-RN Officer Clare Taylor stands by to fire a courtesy salute on the flagship, *Soren Larsen*. Gunpowder is electrically detonated in 1.2 metre long muzzle loading cannons; a sequence of seventeen shots at one minute intervals was the longest salute, fired on entering Santa Cruz de Tenerife. **Bottom:** "Sly" Fox swings out on deck for a cold beer during a hot galley watch in the tropics. The apron says it all!

Above: Like a squadron of men-o'-war breaking the French line at Trafalgar, *Bounty, Tradewind, Amorina* and *Eye of the Wind* heel to a gust on entering Jervis Bay. *Bounty*'s main t'gallant is in the process of being clewed-up and handed. **Bottom left and right:** *Amorina* and *Tradewind* off Point Perpendicular. **Opposite page:** The Fleet at rest in Jervis Bay, sprucing up before arrival in Botany Bay.

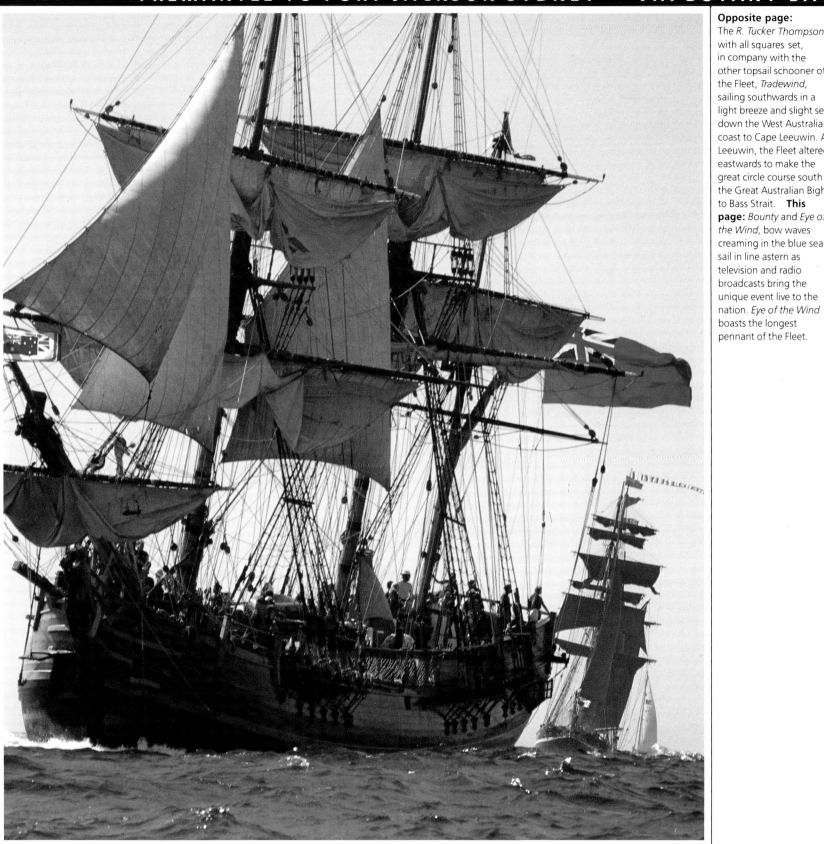

Opposite page:
The *R. Tucker Thompson* with all squares set, in company with the other topsail schooner of the Fleet, *Tradewind*, sailing southwards in a light breeze and slight seas down the West Australian coast to Cape Leeuwin. At Leeuwin, the Fleet altered eastwards to make the great circle course south of the Great Australian Bight to Bass Strait. **This page:** *Bounty* and *Eye of the Wind*, bow waves creaming in the blue sea, sail in line astern as television and radio broadcasts bring the unique event live to the nation. *Eye of the Wind* boasts the longest pennant of the Fleet.

Botany Bay at last! 18 January 1988 — 200 years later to the day after the First Fleet arrived to complete one of the most daring and inspired marine enterprises ever conceived by man.

Soren Larsen is escorted by a Maritime Services Board launch into Botany Bay, leaving Sutherland Point and Captain Cook's landing place to port; Arthur Phillip on HMS *Sirius* had only Cook's charts to guide him. Ferries, yachts, launches, boats, bi-planes, helicopters, light planes and the Royal Australian Navy welcome the Re-enactment Fleet for the bicentennial of the old British colony of New South Wales. In a blustery force 6 southerly, the nine square-riggers sail into the bay with topsails flying, bunting streaming, and the sun shining brilliantly on a pageant of old and new sail.

Sam Gibbs wanted to be the first to enter Botany Bay, and so he raced to the end of the jib-boom (**above**) to claim the honour. For the weary crews of the small vessels, a triumphant parade of sail around the wide bay followed, until the Re-enactment Fleet dropped anchor in the same spot as did the First Fleet in 1788, off Frenchman's Bay.

Bottom: The sails are clewed-up and handed in a harbour stow on top of the yards. In this 19th century rig the clew lines haul the corners of the square sail to the yard ends, while the many buntlines draw up the body of the sail into easily manageable folds. The sausage shapes on the shrouds and stays further aft are "baggy-wrinkles" — anti-chafing gear made from "old stuff" (short ends of rope no good for other uses) to stop wear on the sails.

Above: 0530, first light on 26 January, and a sleepy First Fleet weighs anchor and proceeds seawards for the last time — outward from Botany Bay towards Sydney. **Bottom left:** 0930, outside Sydney Heads. A light easterly breeze wafts the ships into Port Jackson through sea churned white with spectator craft. **Bottom right:** The Harbour Bridge looms into view at last.

Left: *Søren Larsen*'s jib-boom follows the fire tug *Eva Burrows* around Shark and Clarke Islands in the final parade of sail to Farm Cove.
Engineer Brian Broeke, **above**, and nurse Helen Pochojka, **bottom**, two of *Bounty*'s tired crew, happy to have made the long voyage from Sydney's sister city of Portsmouth. One of Brian's first stops ashore will be to visit his tailor.

The full majesty of the world's most beautiful harbour is revealed to the First Fleet Re-enactment ships and crews — with surely one of the greatest welcomes ever given to a fleet of sailing ships. Now numbering the 11 ships of the original Fleet — the Australian-registered *Solway Lass* and *Leeuwin* joined the other 9 for the coastal passage from Botany Bay — the square-riggers almost disappear behind the saluting craft alongside. Over three million people crowded the waters and foreshores of Sydney Harbour, and over 3000 vessels somehow manoeuvred themselves on the sparkling blue waters to give tribute to the ships and crews of the Re-enactment Fleet.

Above: Looking back from the *Søren Larsen*, *Our Svanen*, *One and All*, *Tucker Thompson*, and brown-sailed *Anna Kristina* weave their way between hundreds of boats. **Bottom:** Looking forward from *Bounty*, from left to right, *Our Svanen*, *Tucker Thompson*, *One and All*, *Eye of the Wind*, *Anna Kristina*, *Søren Larsen*, *Amorina*, and *Solway Lass* approach the West German sail-training vessel, *Gorch Fock*, off Elizabeth Bay for her salute.

SAILING HOME

Moored in Farm Cove, 26 January 1988, the ships take pride of place in Australia's 200th birthday celebrations. As HRH the Prince of Wales completed his address to the nation from the steps of the Opera House, the *Søren Larsen* sailed through a curtain of water, her white square-sails set, up to her Farm Cove mooring. The sails were handed in a trice, the bunting hoisted, and HRH was upstaged. His audience turned towards the harbour as, one after the other, the square-riggers appeared around Mrs Macquarie's Point, sailed up to their designated mooring, and so completed the 20,000 nautical mile voyage from the other side of the world. HRH grinned and waved to the scene stealers.

With the passage over and the greatest marine re-enactment ever attempted successfully completed the organisers and crews could relax.

From London, *Søren Larsen*, *R. Tucker Thompson*, *Amorina* and *Tradewind*.

From Portsmouth, *Bounty*, *Anna Kristina* and *Our Svanen*, with *One and All* joining the Fleet in mid-Atlantic.

Eye of the Wind sailed with the Re-enactment ships from Fremantle to Sydney, and *Kaskelot* from London to Portsmouth. Special thanks to the *Lord Nelson*, *Royalist*, *Johanna Lucretia*, *Solway Lass* and *Leeuwin* for adding historical accuracy at Portsmouth and Sydney.

GLOSSARY

ASTERN In, at or towards the rear of a vessel, or in a backwards direction.

BARQUE A sailing vessel, usually three-masted — square-rigged on the first and second masts (foremast and mainmast) and fore and aft rigged on the third mast (the mizzen) (see sail rigging diagram).

BARQUENTINE Similar to a barque but square-rigged on the first or foremast only (see sail rigging diagram).

BEAM The measurement of a ship at its widest part.

BELAYING PIN A removable wooden pin that is slotted in a hole in the pin rail and about which sheets, halyards and braces etc. are made fast.

BLANKETING One sail shielding another from the wind.

BOBSTAY A rope or chain running from the end of the bowsprit to the cutwater, to hold down the bowsprit.

BOWSPRIT The long spar projecting forward over the bow of a sailing ship, mainly to take the stays holding the mast forward. The jib-boom is fastened to the bowsprit and extends forward of it.

BRACE The line from each end of a yard by which the yard is swung or braced around to set the sail to the wind.

BRIG A sailing ship with two square-rigged masts (see sail rigging diagram).

BRIGANTINE Similar to a brig but square-rigged on the first or foremast only (see sail rigging diagram).

CARVEL BUILT A method of construction of a wooden ship, in which the timber planking of the hull is laid edge to edge.

COCK-BILLED When the yards of a vessel are not at right angles to the masts.

COURSE The lowest square sail on any mast of a square-rigged ship.

DAVITS Small cranes for lowering ships' boats.

DEADEYES The traditional wooden block-and-tackle system of tensioning the stays and shrouds of a masted vessel. Now superseded by steel bottle-screws.

DEADLIGHT A shutter of wood or metal for sealing off a cabin window or porthole.

FORE AND AFT SAIL A sail that sets along the length of a vessel rather than across it as in a square rigger.

FOREMAST The first mast behind the bow, when shorter than the second mast.

GAFF A spar holding out the head of a four-sided fore and aft sail.

GASKET A line used to tie a furled sail to a yard.

HALYARD A rope, wire and chain tackle for hoisting and lowering sails, flags and yards.

HANDING Bringing the sail back to its yard, spar or stay in preparation for furling and gasketing.

HERMAPHRODITE BRIG Former name for a brigantine, now generally used to describe a brig that has only main and topmasts on its main or aftermast (see MAST), and no topgallant mast.

HERMAPHRODITE BRIGANTINE A two-masted vessel that has only main and topmasts on its foremast, and no topgallant mast.

JACKSTAFF The pole at the bow of a vessel from which the house-flag on a merchant ship, or national flag on a naval ship, is flown.

JIB-BOOM The spar that projects upwards and outwards from the bowsprit and is supported by the bowsprit.

JIBE Originally, to change direction by accidentally turning the stern through the wind in a square-rigger. When this manoeuvre is carried out purposely it is called "wearing ship".

JURY REPAIRS Makeshift or temporary repairs.

KETCH A two masted fore and aft rigged sailing ship, the aftermast shorter than the forward mast.

KNOT A unit of speed at sea, being one nautical mile per hour.

LLOYD'S OF LONDON An association of merchants and insurance underwriters. The name is from a coffee house in London where the merchants met in 1601.

LLOYD'S REGISTER In 1760 Lloyd's drew up a set of rules regarding the construction of ships for the protection of its underwriters. The Register listed all ships built to those rules and rated them accordingly. A1 at Lloyd's is top classification.

MAIN COURSE The largest square sail on a vessel.

MAINSAIL The largest fore and aft sail on a vessel.

MAST A mast of a vessel — for example, the foremast — traditionally is made up of sections, each section fastened to the one below it i.e. the fore mainmast — the first section above deck; the fore topmast — the second section above deck; the fore topgallant — the third section above deck.

MIZZEN The third mast after the bow.

POOP A short deck over the stern of a ship.

PORT The left side of a ship when facing forward from the stern.

REEFING The operation of shortening a sail by furling it and tying it along the reef points.

REEF POINTS A row of short ropes attached along the body of a sail to allow it to be furled and tied and thus expose less surface to the wind.

REEVE To feed a rope or cable through blocks or eyes to set up a tackle; or to fasten by passing the rope around or through something.

SCHOONER Usually a two masted fore and aft rigged sailing ship, when the main mast, the second mast, is equal to or taller than the fore mast.

SPRITSAIL Originally a small square sail set below and from the bowsprit on square-rigged ships, and now a fore and aft sail set on a sprit or a spar attached to the outer top corner of a sail and fastened to the base of a mast.

STARBOARD The right side of a ship, when facing forward from the stern.

TACK To change direction by turning the bow through the wind.

WATER-SAIL An extra sail, usually set in light winds below the boom or rail of a vessel to catch the wind flowing over the surface of the water.

YARD A spar with tapered ends, hung athwart ships from the mast and used to suspend a square sail. Its name is taken from the section of mast that supports it (see MAST).

The diagram below shows the main working sail areas of a "full-rigged" ship of the clipper type. The standing rigging consists of shrouds and stays that hold up the masts. The running rigging, that operates the setting and movement of the sails, is not shown as it would amount to a maze of over one hundred lines.

1. Spanker.
2. Mizzen course.
3. Mizzen topsail.
4. Mizzen topgallant.
5. Mizzen royal.
6. Main royal.
7. Main topgallant: *sometimes divided into upper and lower topgallant.*
8. Main topsail: *sometimes divided into upper and lower topsail.*
9. Main course.
10. Fore royal.
11. Fore topgallant: *sometimes divided into upper and lower topgallant.*
12. Fore topsail: *sometimes divided into upper and lower topsail.*
13. Fore course.
14. Foresails or jibs.
15. Stay to hold up the mast. *Forestays leading from foremast to bowsprit hold the mast forward.*
16. Bowsprit.
17. Deadeyes (see inset).
18. Jib-boom.
19. Dolphin striker.
20. Transom.
21. Fore mainmast.
22. Fore topmast.
23. Fore topgallant mast.
24. Fore truck.
25. Martingale.
26. Bobstay.
27. Main top: (inset) *mast section junction, shrouds.*

18TH CENTURY BARQUE OR "CAT"

BARQUENTINE

MODERN BRIGANTINE

SQUARE TOPSAIL SCHOONER

GALEAS

MODERN HERMAPHRODITE BRIG

MODERN HERMAPHRODITE BRIGANTINE

SHIP

PERMANENT CREW

Soren Larsen

Tony Davies (UK)	Master
Dan Yates (UK)	First Mate
David Iggulden (UK)	Second Mate
David Mitchell (Australia)	Third Mate
Peter Blackman (UK)	Engineer
John Gryska (USA)	Boatswain
Andy Riley (UK)	Medical Purser
Miranda Kichenside (UK)	AB — (L to T) and (CT to M)
Rob Simpson (Australia)	Deckhand
Clare Taylor (UK)	Deckhand
Paul Franklin (Australia)	Deckhand — (T to M)
Fleur Davies (UK)	Purser
Peter Moore (UK)	Cook
Tisha Cam (UK)	Cook
Tristan Davies (UK)	Ship's boy
Natasha Davies (UK)	Ship's girl

R. Tucker Thompson

Todd Thompson (NZ)	Master — (L to T) and (CT to S)
Russell Harris (NZ)	Master — (T to CT) and (F to S)
Joachim Borgstrom (NZ)	Mate — (all legs except M to F)
Mitch Maciupa (UK)	Mate
Brian Whitford (USA)	Watch Leader — (all legs except CT to M)
Sam Gibbs (Australia)	Watch Leader — (CT to F)
Melanie Harris (NZ)	Deckhand — (T to CT) and (M to S)
Gillian Jean (UK)	Deckhand — (R to M)
Helen Pochojka (UK)	Deckhand — (P to T)

Anna Kristina

John Sorensen (Denmark)	Master
Henrik Nielsen (Denmark)	First Mate — (P to SA)
David Seidl (Canada)	First Mate — (CT to S)
Soren Andreassen (Denmark)	Watch Leader/Boatswain — (P to R)
Marc Seidl (USA)	Second Mate/Boatswain — (CT to S)
Johan Brox (Norway)	Engineer
Salo van de Vooren (Netherlands)	AB
Mons Branstrom (Norway)	AB
Abby Heath (UK)	Purser
Katrine Nordow (Denmark)	Cook/Deckhand
Gillian Jean (UK)	Deckhand — (T to R)

Amorina

Sven Strömberg (Sweden)	Master
Walter Roth (Sweden)	First Mate
Peter Breid (Sweden)	Second Mate
Peter Riddell (Australia)	Third Mate
Bjorn Löfgren (Sweden)	Chief Engineer
Lars Palmgren (Sweden)	First Engineer
Petra Eurenius (Sweden)	Second Engineer
Torbjorn Shulz (Sweden)	Engineer — (L to P) landed by launch, sick
Sigge Gustafsson (Sweden)	Boatswain
Dan Stinson (Australia)	Boatswain — (L to R)
Helena Nillson (Sweden)	Deckhand
Andy Oliver (USA)	Deckhand — (L to R)
Judi Lincoln (Australia)	Deckhand — (L to P)
Bogdan Michalkowski (Australia)	Deckhand — (T to S)
Graeme Speed (Australia)	Deckhand — (R to S)
Carol Zakula (Canada)	Deckhand — (T to S)
Kerstin Ericsson (Sweden)	Purser
Reijo Koikkalainen (Sweden)	Cook — (L to T)
Susanne Hall (Sweden)	Cook — (T to S)
Gillian Jean (UK)	Deckhand — (P to T)

Tradewind

Mark Hammond (NZ)	Master
David Mayhew (UK)	First Mate
Neal "Yakka" Hyde (Australia)	Second Mate/Engineer
Ashley Christie (Australia)	AB
Sam Dean (UK)	AB
Joachim Borgstrom (NZ)	Watch Leader — (M to F)
Adrian Stroes (Netherlands)	AB — (L to M)
Paul Van Os (South Africa)	AB — (CT to M)
Paul Cools (Australia)	AB — (M to S)
Alison Brown (USA)	AB — (L to T) and (CT to M)
Judi Lincoln (Australia)	Purser/Deckhand — (R to S)
Helen Pochojka (UK)	Deckhand — (L to P) and (T to R)
Sue Northcott (NZ)	Deckhand — (L to S)
Rose Northcott (NZ)	Deckhand — (L to M)

One and All

Colin Kesteven (Australia)	Master
Dick Ridsdale (Australia)	First Mate
Mike Hanson (Australia)	Second Mate
Neil Wigan (Australia)	Chief Engineer
Noel Doepel (Australia)	Boatswain
Stephanie Calderwood (Australia)	Nurse
Penny Oxenbridge (Australia)	AB
Andrew Laslett (Australia)	AB
Naomi Howard (Australia)	AB
Ian Judd (NZ)	AB
Lorrae Burke (Australia)	AB
Donald Mitton (Australia)	AB
Kevin Priestly (Australia)	AB
Sylvia Fox (UK)	Cook

Our Svanen

Ken Edwards (Australia)	Master — (M to S)
Jay d'Ambrumenil (Canada)	Sailing Master
Bruce Adam (Australia)	First Mate

Bounty

Ken Edwards (Australia)	Master — (P to R)
Adrian Small (UK)	Master — (R to S)
Peter Smith (Australia)	First Mate — (P to T)
Peter Manthorpe (Australia)	First Mate — (T to S)
Phil Sefton (UK)	Second Mate
Mario Ruel (Canada)	Third Mate/Sailing Master — (P to R)
Bart Terwiel (Canada)	Purser/Third Mate
David Lewis (UK)	Chief Engineer
Brian Broeke (Canada)	Second Engineer
David Atkins (UK)	Third Engineer
David Keenan (UK)	Electrical Engineer — (R to M)
Mike Davidson (Australia)	Radio Operator
Sam Gibbs (Australia)	Boatswain — (P to R)
Dan Stinson (Australia)	Boatswain — (R to S)
David Nash (Australia)	Shipwright
Anthony Owen (Australia)	AB — (P to M) and (F to S)
Mark Abbott (UK)	AB — (R to F)
Richard Grissel (Australia)	Deck Cadet — (R to S)
Keith Hornsblow (UK)	Ship's Boy — (R to S)
Judi Lincoln (Australia)	Deckhand — (P to R)
Helen Pochojka (UK)	Deckhand — (R to S)
Julian Martelli (Australia)	Cook — (P to R)
Miranda Kichenside (UK)	Cook — (T to CT)
Karen Guardenier (USA)	Cook — (R to S)
Toni Hutchinson (Australia)	Assistant Cook (P to R)
Kerri Mills (UK)	Assistant Cook — (R to CT)
Jo Whitehead (Australia)	Assistant Cook — (R to S)

Eye of the Wind

Tim Gellatly (Australia)	Master
Tony "Tiger" Timbs (UK)	Sailing Master
Dave Brown (Australia)	First Mate
Ray Cummings (Australia)	Watch Leader
Liam Walsh (UK)	Watch Leader
Peter Kane (NZ)	Engineer
Robin Hicks (Australia)	Boatswain
Kevin Taylor (UK)	Boatswain's Mate
Deborah Heyden (Australia)	Purser
Helen Bird (UK)	Cook
Tams Norrison (Australia)	Assistant Cook

TRAINEE CREW

London to Portsmouth
5 ships

Søren Larsen
Brian McKenzie
Roger Fenry
Jonathan King
Jane King
Lowana King
Bryony King
Millie King
Jason Clarke
Sam Crossley
Bill Condie
Gary Jacobs
Alan Garth
David Minchin
Harold Moss
Herbert Bentley

Amorina
Victoria Solt
Peggy Krementz
Ian Reith
Gordon Carvosso
Donald Halliwell
Richard Tanner
Lyn Tanner
Patrick Davis
Anne von Bertouch
Ann Schooler
Neridah Brandstatler
Donald Neighbour
Carol Thatcher
Ley Goodwin
Richard Miller
James Bingham
Eskett Hazen
Magdaline Wheeler
James Wheeler
Reginald Terry
John Kuetemeyer
Clare Bewsher
Warren Michael
Don Sandgrove
Julie Abnett
Lance Trendall

Ian Graham
Bernard Brandstater
George Wood
William Haller
Judith Lincoln
Justine Wilford
Marcus Mainwaring
Graham Lipscombe
Patricia Gaynor
Nanu Irvine
Bill Cross
Srantz Gawell

Kaskelot
(Permanent Crew and Trainees)
Tommi Nielson
Rob Morton
David Caine
Dan Stinson
David McQueen
Sarah White
Dominic Dev Wills
Peter Veen
Alan Dunbell
Andrea Oliver
Caroline Eltringham
Sam Deer
Jochen Howell
Rob Stratton
Brian James

R. Tucker Thompson
Peter Gardner
Frank Chatfield
Angela Lind
Douglas Marshland
Nancy Clare
Brian Brady

Tradewind
Alison Brown
Fred Pentecost

Portsmouth to Tenerife
6 trainee ships plus **Our Svanen**

Søren Larsen
Nigel Hopkins
Anthony Lewis
Anne von Bertouch
Anthony Curtis
Chris Fox
Roger Lean Vercoe
Hyman Warmbath
John Ellicott
Donald Halliwell
Alan Kay
Dario Carballo
Trevor Redpath
John Lind
John Gandy
Alan Garth
William Leimbach
Jonathan King
Geoffrey Lyon

Amorina
Valma Steward
Bruno Bockli
Gordon Carvosso
Marcus Mainwaring
Peggy Knight
Kenneth Allblom
Margaret Holt
Diana Mitchell
Derick Johnston
Bryan Thompson
Frank Ibbott
Bruce Menzies
Kevin Clarke
John Clarke
Gary Roberts
Vilhelm Sohlberg
Wenzel Kropacek
Bernice Hooker

Anna Kristina
Bill Walker
Stefan Grumbach
Susanne Grumbach

Clare Puntis
Abby Heath
Roy Jones

Bounty
David Blackley
Douglas Marstand
Robert Owen
William Robertson
Richard Clarke
H. Parsons
Brett Weeks
Robert Ilgner
George Wood
Walter Bresinger
Peter Blasey
Robin Terry
Curgie Pratt
Helena Cora
Ken Roseberry

R. Tucker Thompson
Brian Brady
Ann Schooler
Ken Stewart
Juliet Stewart
Adrian Wakenshaw

Tradewind
Anthony Davidson
Stephen McInnes
Duncan Reed
William Cooper
F. Winterbottom
John Gandy
Janet Butterworth
Alison Brown
Fred Pentecost

Tenerife to Rio de Janeiro
6 trainee ships plus **Our Svanen**

Søren Larsen
Ann Schooler
Edwin Murphy
Jason Elsworth
Alan Forsyth
Paul Franklin
Tony Jeffree
Anthony Curtis
Alan Garth
Bill Leimbach
Duncan Reed
Clare Puntis
Deborah Bass
Geoffrey Lyon
Robert Oyston
Anne von Bertouch
Chris Fox
Jonathan King

Amorina
Jack Mortimer
George Glaister
Marjorie Glaister
Arne Mellgren
John Ellicott
Paul Richter
Jo Bell-Chamber
John Niles
Kayla Niles
Margaret Holt
Peter Simpson-Jones
Bogdan Michalkowski
Arthur Britton
Charlotte Thamo
Peter Riddell
Fred Pentecost
Carol Zakula
Martin Olving
Malcolm Clarke

Anna Kristina
Gordon Carvosso
William Cooper
John Dempster

Bill Walker
Tricia McCue
Garry Nicholson
John Lind
Marcus Mainwaring
Gillian Jean

Bounty
Charlotte Broughton
Terence Wing
John Rivett
Peggy Dare
Nerida Stark
Robert Brooks
Bonnie McKenzie
Bruce Mellor
Liz Hutson
William Holmes
David Blackmore
David Blackley
Loly Cora
Helena Cora
Bruce Fogan

R. Tucker Thompson
Kent Clift
Stephen Mundell
Stephen Herbert
Emma Smallwood
Jimmy Skoog
Jacky Sugden

Tradewind
Andy Clarke
Lynn Scott
Lynette Diffey
Stephen McInnes
Robin Grigg
Roelof Brouwer
Aleida Leeuwenberg

Rio de Janeiro to Cape Town

6 trainee ships plus **Our Svanen**

Søren Larsen
Wendy Newton
Paul Franklin
Ian Hutchinson
Jack Perrin
Paul LeFort
Samuel Harvey
Malcolm Clarke
Anne Knowles
Peter Ellicott
Vivian Webster
Jennifer Ehmann
Craig Dandeaux
Chris Fox
Bill Leimbach
Tony Curtis
Roelof Brouwen
Anne von Bertouch
Stephen Mundell

Susanne Phillips
Mark Bewell
Ricardo Neto
Armando Hello
Fasin Achilles

Bounty
Anthony Owen
Fleur Ball
Charlotte Broughton
Jim Kelly
Joy Kelly
Deborah Laird
Ric Robinson
John Robinson
Alan Sangster
Andrew Urban
Roger Fyfe
Tim Stark
Richard Grissel
Ann Schooler
Keith Hornsblow
Thomas Webster
Mark Abbott
Jonathan King
Jo Whitehead

Amorina
David Haynes
James Grigg
Ingrid Kammerer
Carol Sparre
Michael Keats
Mark Leach
Fred Pentecost
Lindsey Tuck
Margaret Holt
Kenneth Darby
Gordon Carvosso
Timothy Miller
Rory Mainwaring
Marcus Mainwaring
Clare Puntis
Bill Cooper
John Lind
Graeme Speed
Lilian Tschabold

Anna Kristina
Loly Cora
Leigh Park

R. Tucker Thompson
Duncan Reed
Graham Godden
Bernadette O'Rielly
Goncalo De Macedo
Patrick Verbeck
Gillian Jean

Tradewind
Helena Cora
Lyn Diffey
Evelyn Brown
Alex Rayment
Shane Bobilak
Gary Blanchard
Andrea Oliver

Cape Town to Mauritius

7 ships plus **Our Svanen**

Søren Larsen
Anne von Bertouch
Chris Fox

Paul Franklin
Susan Beharriell
Berenice Hooker

Wayne Bendall
Graham Brown
Glen Krause
Peter McKenzie
Robert Weekly
Terrance Williams
Susan Robson
Denise O'Neill
Peter Foster
Lynnogan Foster
Spencer Sandilands
Annette Parkes

Amorina
Raymond Job
Donald Whitewood
Richard Bisset
Edward James
Ian Westley
C. Paul
Rory Mainwaring
Marcus Mainwaring
Jim Grigg
Gordon Carvosso
Ingrid Kammerer
Bill Cooper
Fred Pentecost
Dr Alastair Reid
Timothy Mace
Keith Miller
Patricia Gordon
Peter Simpson-Jones
Clare Puntis
Robert Bradshaw
Adrian Jackson
Susan Baddeley
Bill Jory
Ann Finnegan
Margaret Holt
Jean Boin
Heather Ohlssen
Christian Ohlssen
Bill Adeny
Jim Maloney
Gordon Geraghty
Charles Follington
Maureen Forbes
Raymond Woff
Stephen Ashley
Evelyn Brown
 Shirley Hurlstone-Jones

Anna Kristina
Mark Seidl
David Seidl
Johan Mustad
Niels Rómeling
John Stevens
Ann Schooler
Peter Goy

Bounty
Fleur Ball
John Glasser
Roger Fyfe
Cassandra Eustace
Margaret Lindsmith
Michael Wood
Christioph Oliver
William Dieter
Roberto Manuzzi
John Edye
Bruce Rosenberg
Oliver Halley
Jo Whitehead
Gavin Fox
Linda Wollstein
Oliver Rennert
Michael Glasser
Dieter Vogt
Keith Hornsblow
Richard Grissel
Mark Abbott

One and All
Tracey Rowan
Edwin Shearer
Richard Kuhn
Mark Leach
Brian Critchley
Stephen Mundell
John Hatton
Stephen Piercy
Helena Cora
Charlotte Broughton
Michael Keats
Tony Curtis
Kerry Brewster
Michael Balson
Malcolm Clarke
Jonathan King
Andrea Oliver

R. Tucker Thompson
Robert Bell
Derek Morton
Eric Janes
Gillian Jean
Ian Hutchinson
Paul LeFort
Ross Ridgway-Pearce
Kim Saville

Tradewind
Charles Gilbert
Michael Gibson
Randall Archer
Douglas Bean
Peter van der Meer
Duncan Reed
Alison Brown
Paul van Os

Mauritius to Fremantle

8 trainee ships

Søren Larsen
Annette Parkes
Anne von Bertouch
Chris Fox
Tony Curtis
Michael Balson
Jonathan King
Gary Jacobs
John Edwards
Robbin Grossky
Kerryn Macauley
Jennifer Overton
Judi Halpin
Judi Bethell
Dawn Sutton
Don Sutton
Louise Bratt
Edward Coleridge
Jerry Griffiths
Peter Howe
Tom Ball
John Green
Duncan Reed
Ian James
Peter Chapman
Sophie Lagesse

Amorina
Margaret Holt
Marcus Mainwaring
Ingrid Kammerer
Bill Cooper
Donald Whitewood
William Adeny
Mary Guest
Lizbeth Hodes
Digby Hughes
John Bartle
Baljit Sidhu
Franzes Dalziel
Margaret Anton
Harvard Hawkins
Robert Adeny
Terence O'Keefe
Jonathan Warren
Robert Inns
Robert Messenger
Jacqueline Wallbank
Colin Brigstock
Janice Ray
Mark Hanlon
Paul Kirkman
Joan Ponton
Eric Ponton
Helen Sen

Joan Hale
Sandra Sleeman
Daryl Frunks
Karen Pike
Allan Jamieson
Shirley Koessig
Yvonne Whitewood
John Fraser
Christine Place
Andrew Stockford
Francis Rice
Allan White
David Askey
Rodger Hutchings
James McGregor
Clifford Pilon
Phillip Cook
Christopher Ryan
Nerida Stark

Anna Kristina
George Camille
Helga Richard
Philip Smith
William Nandris
Jane Utting
Patricia Martin
Kevin Gibson
Robert Gluckman
Darice Eckburg
Mark Leach
David Short
Johan Mustad
Sue Northcott
Shirley Hurlstone-Jones
Gillian Jean
Grant Philpott
Phil Smith
Diana Broad

Bounty
Craig Douglas
Michael Sigston
Roger Fyfe
James Parbery
Catherine Williams
Jeffrey Waters
Michael Evans
Daniel Enright
Kenneth George
C. Netrebenko
Ron Mapledoram
Alan Bateman
Peter Galton
Mary Manigan

Richard Niven
Garry Maloney
Harry Morcom
Catherine Stockwood
Lucy Maddison
Mark Barrington
Stanley Birkett
DeeDee Ferguson

One and All
Tracey Rowan
Daniel Macleod
Albert Meester
Trevor Gadd
Cyril McLeod
Peter Telcher
Susan Pockley
William Tomlinson
Steven Rybalka
Charlotte Broughton
Therese Toohey
Marjorie Mort
Ann Schooler
Elizabeth Ayris
Wilfred Martin
Colin Poad
Marc Gilmour
Peter Shaddock
Garry Danswan
Stanley Rayner
Leslie Hole
Jessica Wade
Peter Milne
Peter Goy
Ronald Burton
Craig Dandeaux
Jennifer Ehmann
Bruce Smith
Clare Puntis
John Feather

Our Svanen
Karen Barr

Fremantle to Sydney

9 ships

Søren Larsen
Jennifer Overton
Duncan Reed
Elizabeth Forbes
Jocelyn Forbes
Walter Romanes
Ronald M'oo
Chris Egan
Annette Parkes
Neal Russell

Simon Dawe
Gary McBride
Rod Sutherland
Cedric Bullard
Graham Smedley
Martha Gledhill
Jaap Fabery de Jonge
Paul LeFort
Anne Young
Neils Romeling

R. Tucker Thompson
Richard Bewell
Gregory Cozens
Margaret Fay
Sarah Adams
Gregory McKay
Sam Samuelson
Gavin Fox
Oliver Rennet
Ross Ridgeway-Pearce

Tradewind
Carolyn Badger
Jean Johnston
Brian Bourne
Wesley Baker
Phillip Lambert
Johann Krestyn
Kathryn Henthorn
Christopher Paul
Christine Lane
Sandra Hansell
Rowan Humphrey
Colin Watson
John Callahan
John Paterson
Lyn Diffey
Tony Allen
Steven Johnson
Ewan Warmbath
Maurice Champion
Robina Champion

Sophia Lagesse
Geoffrey Carroll
Chris Fox
Jonathan King
Elizabeth Blake
Bill Forbes
Clare Puntis
Tony Curtis
Anne von Bertouch
Margaret Holt

Charles Rixon
Liz Hodes
Barbara Cam
Rona Capp
Lucinda Dennison
Thomas Bell

Amorina
Hendrikus van Gool
David Phillips
William Adeney
Kelly Hensley
Pamela Phelan
Edgar Adams
Thomas Gould
Hugh Bradly
Keith Forster
Frank Bawden
George Kapetas
Stephen Baddeley
Art Hislop
Tina Straatmans
Robert Griffiths
Darrin Laing
Loraine Lincoln
Silvia Russell
Anthony Russell
Cassandra Russell
Fred Andrews
Susan Nixon
Anne Byrnes
Nicholas Panos
Verona Wolfensberger
Stanley Parsonage
Joe Dundas
Stephen Kiefer
Kenneth Warburton
John Taylor
William Head
Ernest Steel
Jonathan Whitehead
Heinrich Lubcke
Graeme Quarford
Betty Gehrig
Gordon Carvosso
John Fraser
Allan Jamieson
Shirley Koessig
Jacqueline Wallbank
Joan Hale
Frances Dalziel
Yvonne Whitewood
W. Miersch
H. Miersch
Julia Pitt
Marion Ham

Anna Kristina
John Green
Ian Bottomley
Sam Davies

Malcolm Grant
Marcus Mainwaring
Mats Huss
Wayne Bishop
Helga Richard
Jane Utting
Patricia Martin
Glen Short
Johan Mustad
Helena Cora
John Colville

Bounty
Kathleen Stutsel
John Bartle
Roberta Cole
Pam Carland
Lionel Davidson
Robert Lewandowski
John Lloyd
Mary Manigian
Catherine Williams
Colin Wright
Peter Pethabridge
George Wood
Oliver Rennet
Constantine Netrebenko
Michael Evans
Craig Griffin
John Wrold
Ruth Hablethwaite
Katrina Faulkes
Mary Bush
Ted Hawes
Andrew Macleod
Vincent Metham
David Blackmore
Michael Morgan
John Wrout

Eye of the Wind
Richard Bewell
Brian Bourne
Cedric Bullard
Timothy Cecil
Rachel Cecil
Nicholas Cox
Rene Dan
Mark Hanlon
Carla Horne
Paul Kirkman
James McGregor
Robert Milton
Cliff Pilon
Janice Ray
Niels Roemeling
Gillian Jean
Phillip Lambert

One and All
Joanna Adams

Alqis Bacter
Steven Bowden
Dr F. Bremke
Bernard Brandstater
Jenny Cambell
Garry Danswan
V. Doepel
Ray Edmiston
Alan Fulcher
H. J. Graham
M. Ham
Anthony Hembling
Michael Houston
Robert Johnson
Jennifer Johnson
Pauline Kehoe
York Loffler
John Loudon
Jane Lovell
Phillip Lynch
Daniel Macleod
Kathryn Mahon
Rosemary Mahon
Albert Meester
Chris Ryan
Aubyn Schafer
Peter Telcher
Therese Toohey
Martin Wood

Our Svanen
Ann Schooler
Michaela Hill
Ann Montgomery
Darren Booy
Mark Ainsworth
Richard Mainwaring
Rose Richter
Ray Holland
Michael Molesworth
Gary McBride
Arthur Ward
Peter Davey
Colleen Taylor
Roger Kent
Rod Sutherland
Breda Annesley
A. Buisman
Mark Clifford
Tanya Engvig
David Stewart
Donald Goodsir
Annalise Penfold
Brian Whelan
Matthew Hunter

R. Tucker Thompson
Lynette Diffey
Norm Croker
Roy Forbes
Geoffrey Nixon

John Perry
Sharron Perry
Miranda Stewart
Jim Wintour

Tradewind
Suzanne Adams
Michael Archnial
Carolyn Badger
Wesley Baker
Trevor Bailey
Julien Burnside
Richard Conibear
Peter Dind
Ulrich Furer
Murray Hodge
Linda Layton
Ernest Magee
Catherine O'Reilly
Meredith Osbourne
Joche Pitt
Gerhard Puschter
Maxwell Rumble
Dorothy Smith
Rick Turvey
Charles Tye

FIRST FLEET PERSONNEL

At Sea

Captain Mike Kichenside (UK),
Commodore . . . . *Søren Larsen*

Captain Ken Edwards (Australia),
Vice-Commodore . . . . *Bounty/Our Svanen*

Rob Simpson (Australia),
Fleet Surgeon . . . . *Søren Larsen*

David Iggulden (UK),
Fleet Communications . . . . *Søren Larsen*

Peter Riddell (Australia),
Deputy Fleet Surgeon . . . . *Amorina/Tradewind*

Clare Taylor (UK),
Fleet Purser . . . . *Søren Larsen*

Gillian Jean (UK),
Fleet Dentist . . . . *Anna Kristina/Amorina/R. Tucker Thompson/*
Our Svanen/Eye of the Wind

Judi Lincoln (Australia),
Fleet Nurse and Children's Education Officer . . . . *Tradewind/Bounty/Amorina*

Helen Pochojka (UK),
Fleet Nurse . . . . *Bounty/R. Tucker Thompson/Tradewind*

Bill Liembach (USA)
Tony Curtis (Australia)
Mike Bolsom (Australia)
Fleet Film and Documentary Crew . . . . *Søren Larsen/Bounty/*
One and All/R. Tucker Thompson/Our Svanen/Amorina/Anna Kristina/Tradewind

Malcolm Clarke (UK)
Fleet Photographer . . . . *Søren Larsen/Bounty/*
One and All/R. Tucker Thompson/Our Svanen/Amorina/Anna Kristina/Tradewind

Paul Franklin (Australia),
Ship/Shore Operations . . . . *Søren Larsen*

Sue Northcott (NZ)
Rose Northcott (NZ)
Ship/Shore Support . . . . *Tradewind/Anna Kristina/R. Tucker Thompson*

Dr Jonathan King (Australia),
Project Founder and Creative Director . . . . *Søren Larsen/Bounty/One and All*

Shore Support

Wally Franklin (Australia),
Executive Director

Mark Crittle (Australia),
Shore Operations Manager

Gerry Weingarth (Australia),
Liaison Officer